SECRETS OF

OF

SATURN

About the Author

Andrea Taylor (Dorset, England) has been an astrological counselor for over forty years. Originally self-taught, she studied through the Huber School in the mid-1980s. She started teaching birth chart interpretation soon after, and she's had clients worldwide. Andrea also authored *The Astrology Book*, *Birth Chart Interpretation Plain & Simple*, *What's Your Big Three?*, and *Secrets of Your Rising Sign*.

SECRETS

OF

SATURN

Decipher
Its Messages
to Take Control
of Your Life

ANDREA TAYLOR

LLEWELLYN
WOODBURY, MINNESOTA

FIRST EDITION
First Printing, 2025

Book design by Samantha Peterson
Cover design by Shira Atakpu
Interior illustrations by Llewellyn Art Department

Llewellyn Publications is a registered trademark of Llewellyn Worldwide Ltd.

Library of Congress Cataloging-in-Publication Data (Pending)
ISBN: 978-0-7387-7934-8

Llewellyn Worldwide Ltd. does not participate in, endorse, or have any authority or responsibility concerning private business transactions between our authors and the public.

All mail addressed to the author is forwarded but the publisher cannot, unless specifically instructed by the author, give out an address or phone number.

Any internet references contained in this work are current at publication time, but the publisher cannot guarantee that a specific location will continue to be maintained. Please refer to the publisher's website for links to authors' websites and other sources.

Llewellyn Publications
A Division of Llewellyn Worldwide Ltd.
2143 Wooddale Drive
Woodbury, MN 55125-2989
www.llewellyn.com

Printed in the United States of America

Other Books by Andrea Taylor

The Astrology Book

Birth Chart Interpretation Plain & Simple

What's Your Big Three?

Secrets of Your Rising Sign

For my lovely husband, whose unfailing support, humour, adventurous spirit, and old-fashioned chivalry show that four planets in Scorpio are not to be feared!

"We do not take a trip; a trip takes us."
—JOHN STEINBECK,
*TRAVELS WITH CHARLEY:
IN SEARCH OF AMERICA*

Contents

Introduction

There haven't been many books written about Saturn, maybe because it seems far more fun to read about our sun, moon, and rising signs or the sort of partner we might get! There is so much to see in a chart; who looks at Saturn? More importantly, who really understands what it is saying? It certainly is a tough planet. Yet, after decades of chart interpretations, I've come to the realisation that we have been interpreting it incorrectly ever since Galileo observed the planet in 1610.

New theories don't appear overnight. My research was sparked by that age-old quest to know what life's purpose is. Having already discovered that the rising sign is part of that spiritual message (check out my book *Secrets of Your Rising Sign*), I knew there must be more in the chart to guide and direct us. It took a lot of research and thought before I realised that Saturn was the answer.

To make sure of my facts, I trawled back through charts I'd done in the 1970s right up to recent ones, and a pattern soon emerged. As I often say, our birth charts hold all the answers, but we have to ask the right questions. Until now, no one has looked to Saturn as a guide to our life path. But the moment I seriously studied the concept, it all fell into place.

I'm now ready to present my new theory on interpreting Saturn. In this book, I aim to change eons-old perceptions of this maligned planet by introducing my revolutionary interpretation in a way I hope everyone can understand, not just professional astrologers. For a long while, I've seen birth charts as maps of our lives (in fact, I was the one who coined the phrase), and after more than forty years, I've finally found the key to our purpose here on Earth, just waiting in our birth charts to be revealed. And that key is Saturn!

As you continue to read, it's important to have your birth chart close by so you can check what your Saturn placement is saying to you. If you don't already have a copy of your birth chart, there are many sites online that will create one for free. Websites will ask for your time, date, and place of birth. It is really important to know the correct time within five or ten minutes; otherwise, your chart may not be accurate.

If you are fairly new to astrology, there is an appendix at the end of the book that explains the astrological terms and concepts that will appear here. It would be a good idea to read that before you start. Alternatively, you could buy my book *Birth Chart Interpretation Plain & Simple*, which will teach you how to interpret your own chart even if you have no prior knowledge.

one
Saturn, Past and Present

In this chapter, I will be exploring Saturn's interpretations through the ages before introducing my new theory. Please don't skip this background information no matter how much previous knowledge you have of Saturn, as it explains the progression of our understanding and interpretation of Saturn as well as how I came to develop my new theory.

A Bit of History About Saturn

Way back in the mists of time, the Romans worshipped a god named Saturn. He was the most revered of all their gods, and they dedicated a temple to him on the most important hill in Rome. The Greeks also had their mythical

Saturn god, whom they called Cronus. Their mythology stated that Zeus exiled Cronus from Olympus, so he went on to rule over Italy and taught his people agriculture. These Greek and Roman myths have become entwined over time, leaving confusion over the exact nature of what Saturn stood for, but it was believed he was the god of time, abundance, wealth, agriculture, renewal, and freedom from restriction.

Roman society was one of strict rules and regulations, but on the festival of Saturnalia—generally held between December 17–23—those rules were set aside and everyone was allowed to relax and have fun. This was a time of excessive eating and drinking and gift-giving. After the fall of the Roman empire, the traditions continued as what we now know as Christmas. Yes, Saturn rules Christmas! Saturn was also celebrated as the god of farming and harvest. Farming is closely linked to the seasons, which flower and fade continually, so Saturn's link with time has continued while other aspects have changed. Today, we don't view Saturn as loosening restrictions for humans nor do we see him as in any way abundant—quite the reverse!

When the planet Saturn was observed by Galileo, the great astronomer of his age, astrologers decided to call it Saturn after the Roman mythological god. Saturn was then assigned as the ruler of both Capricorn and Aquarius. In those days our ability to see the planets was limited, so some of the astrological signs shared a ruling planet: Mars ruled both Aries and Scorpio until Pluto was discovered, and Jupiter ruled both Pisces and Sagittarius until Neptune was seen. Each time a new planet was identified, it was assigned one of the signs awaiting their own planet. When Uranus was discovered in 1781, it was assigned to be the ruler of Aquarius, so Saturn became the lone ruler of Capricorn. Today, some signs still share a ruling planet: Mercury rules both Gemini and Virgo, and Venus rules Taurus and Libra. This raises the question of whether or not even more planets are waiting to be discovered.

Fifty years after Saturn's discovery, William Lilley, the renowned London astrologer of the day, described Saturn in great detail in his book *Christian Astrology*, calling people ruled by it "envious, covetous, jealous and mistrustful, timorous, sordid, outwardly dissembling, sluggish, suspicious, stubborn, contemptuous of women, liars, malicious, never contented."[1] It's hard to see how he could justify this description. Nevertheless, it was the accepted view of the times. The only positives Lilley could find were wisdom and self-discipline. How and why this change in perception of Saturn came about—this alteration from a benign, much-worshipped god into one so maligned by Lilley—is lost in time.

1. William Lilley, *Christian Astrology*, 3rd ed. (Regulus Publishing, 1985), 58.

Three hundred years later, Saturn somehow again metamorphosised into something equally feared but at least believable when C. G. Jung, the famous psychoanalyst, wrote his *Memories, Dreams, Reflections*. His description of Saturn is more in keeping with our modern take:

> Saturn is the most maligned and feared god, for with him comes consciousness of age, sickness, incapacity, and the inevitability of endings. Saturn is also the taskmaster, disciplinarian and teacher whose gifts come rather like curses, leaden with the weight of suffering and guilt. Yet it is Saturn who brings mastery, wisdom, patience, a sense of legacy and history, wealth through endurance, authority and sovereignty, the diamond body that emerges from coal, the gold transmuted from lead.[2]

Saturn's Place in Modern Astrology

Even though our astrological understanding has moved on apace since those very early days of Saturn's discovery, astrologers today still view Saturn very much as Jung described it. Prior to Jung's insights, a birth chart was used as a tool for prediction. In Lilley's day people would

2. C. G. Jung, *Memories, Dreams, Reflections* (Pantheon Books, 1963), 335.

have sought his advice on questions like who they would marry, if they would have money, if a ship would make port, when they would die, etc.

After that period, and until the middle of the last century, astrology fell out of fashion. Even in the early 1970s when I was starting to study it, astrology was considered nonsense by the majority of people—and still is by some. But when Linda Goodman's brilliant sun sign book, simply titled *Sun Signs*, became a bestseller (probably the only astrology book that's ever managed that!), a lot more people started talking about astrology, and the first thing we all did at parties was exchange our sun sign information.

By the 1980s, looking at a birth chart from a psychological perspective had astrologers afire with enthusiasm. This was mostly thanks to Bruno and Louise Huber, who came up with their method of psychological astrology. This involved using a chart as a psychological tool rather than simply as a means of prediction.

Psychology requires us to talk about our feelings, and this became the norm of the 1980s. Expressing our feelings was something previously frowned upon—certainly here in the UK, where we were still expected to maintain that "stiff upper lip." I can clearly recall hearing that in America, many people were attending counselling in an effort to make sense of their lives. As fashions and expressions that start in America eventually find their way to the UK (and vice versa), within a few years it also became acceptable for us in the UK to talk about inner emotions.

Even so, it made little difference to how we interpreted Saturn in our charts. Saturn has always been seen as the fear area. Although we were newly encouraged to openly express our inner fears, it was still believed we became stronger as individuals if we confronted them head-on. We were actively encouraged to go towards the area of life Saturn was in, draw our sword, and do battle—to slay the enemy within.

Liz Greene wrote an amazingly insightful and learned book on Saturn back in 1976, titled *Saturn: A New Look at an Old Devil.* Her descriptions of the difficulties Saturn presents in the elements, signs, and houses are still the best interpretations I've come across. But her slant was psychological, not spiritual, and it, too, gave advice on overcoming these constraints.

Saturn's Spiritual Role and My New Theory

My belief is that we are now moving into a whole new era of spiritual awareness. We want to know our life purpose; why we are here. A birth chart holds the answer to that question, but we have to look at it from a new perspective. I'm calling this *spiritual astrology*.

My previous book, *Secrets of Your Rising Sign*, explained the first level of this new spiritual interpretation: that our rising sign was our sun sign in our previous life. Saturn, too, is assuming a very different role in light of this new theory, and he is neither that benign god of Roman myth nor the feared task-master of later centuries.

I submit a new theory that Saturn is placed in an area you are not supposed to go—which I will refer to as the "no-go area" for simplicity's sake—and this is why we face so many restrictions in that area. Also, I believe there is a karmic/cosmic reason for this.

This is not idle speculation. In all my consultations over the years, not one of my clients had overcome their associated fear of the area Saturn inhabited. This made me question Saturn's role, and the more I looked, the more obvious it became that we have been viewing its message incorrectly. I talked with many clients, past and present, and my new theory proved itself right in every case.

I realised our view of Saturn needed revising because life gives us plenty of other opportunities for self-growth and enlightenment. Quite frankly, life is tough enough. So why would we want to do battle with an enemy that is determined to win? Because Saturn has to win. Saturn's role is to prevent us from going down a blind alley, one we are not meant to be heading down—no way is it going to allow us to access it. If we attempt to knock down the road blocks to that area of life, we can have some access; after all, we do have a certain amount of free will and free choice. But, in time, we will reach a brick wall and be forced to do a U-turn, ending up right back where we started.

If we accept that Saturn is indeed in a no-go zone, how can we discover where we are supposed to be heading? My investigations have always led back to three aspects in particular that we must take note of when analysing Saturn's coded message.

1. The Position of the Sun: The House and the Sign It Occupies

Apart from the sign the sun is in (which shows the manner in which we use the sun's energy), it's really important to note the house. This is the area of life we are being asked to direct the sun's energy. Even more importantly, is it above or below the ascendant/descendant (AC/DC) line?

This is another new idea, so let's concentrate on understanding this concept. Imagine a line being drawn from the AC to the DC, across the chart from left to right. Think of this line as the *horizon line*. There are now two halves: the top and the bottom.

There is more detail about this in the following chapters, but briefly, my theory is that if the sun is below the horizon line in houses one through six, this life is one of service to others. The rewards that come in this life are not just material; they are also spiritual. This often indicates someone who is an old soul, a person who has chosen this path to lead to higher enlightenment. Therefore, having the sun below the horizon line usually predicts a life that is unseen in a worldly sense. While this life will not be lived in the public eye, it is no less important to those whose lives are enhanced by the individual's selfless service.

If the sun is above the AC/DC line in houses seven through twelve, we are meant to shine in one way or another. The sun here means that individuals will have their own ideas, thoughts, actions, and motivations, and their task is to bring something to mankind. The top of the chart is also the place of humanitarian ideals. People who inhabit this area of the chart bring change to others' lives in a myriad of ways.

2. What Your North Nodes Are Telling You About Your Life Path

In all of the clients I have worked with over the years, I've noticed that none of them have any desire to interact with the house (area of life) their north node sits in, whereas they do resonate strongly with the south node house. This is because we lived in this south node area in our previous life, so it is familiar and comfortable to us.[3]

But life is about growth, which is often uncomfortable. The north and south nodes explain both where we came

3. My book *Secrets of Your Rising Sign* looks at the south node in detail.

from and where we should be heading in this life. They are very important spiritual markers. Although we typically don't want to go towards the north node area, life will gradually guide us there. There is no need to take any conscious action; it happens over a lifetime in small shifts and changes. The key is not to cling too tightly to the past—allow yourself to be led.

It is worth remembering that the doors that are meant to open do so, whereas if we are on the wrong path, they will remain firmly locked. This is frustrating and upsetting because humans often want what we are not meant to have, and acceptance is one of the hardest spiritual lessons. There is more information on these ideas in the following chapters.

3. The Quadrant Emphasis:
Where Are Most of Your Planets?

Rather like the sun's position in a birth chart, the quadrant emphasis shows us where to direct our life force. If you've never come across the idea of separating a chart into quadrants (sections), halves, and sides, it would be best to familiarise yourself before continuing; there is a section on this in the appendix. The quadrants are an important part of understanding my new theory about Saturn's role.

When we go against the message of the quadrant emphasis, it usually results in failure because we are not on the right path. For example, if most of your planets are at the bottom of the chart (called *the collective*), endeavouring to stand out as an individual by expressing yourself at the top of the chart will fail. We tend to think of failure as some fault of our own, but in fact, we often fail because we have strayed from the correct path. The "failure" is redirecting us where we are meant to be.

If you don't already have some understanding of these important aspects of astrology—the sun by sign and house, the north nodes, and the quadrants—it would be a good idea to learn more about them before going further, because I'll be referencing them throughout the book. Check out my book *Birth Chart Interpretation Plain & Simple* for easy but detailed explanations, or read the appendix at the back of the book for a brief overview.

In the following chapters, I will explain how Saturn affects the house (area of life) it is in, starting with the elements (fire, earth, air, and water). Although I'm introducing a new way of interpreting Saturn, the fact remains that it still affects each sign and house negatively, and we will feel this as we always have: as a fear area, and as a place we don't want to go. It is important to fully understand how Saturn affects each sign and house before delving into why it is there, especially before looking at its coded messages regarding our own cosmic/soul path.

two
Saturn in the Elements

This chapter will provide a brief overview of how Saturn acts in the astrological signs, based initially on their element: whether the sign is a fire, earth, air, or water sign.

Saturn in the Fire Signs:
Aries, Leo, and Sagittarius

The fire signs are traditionally very difficult places for Saturn. Fire represents drive, energy, enthusiasm for action, and new beginnings. It's our expression of ourselves at every level. Aries is about who we are as individuals, Leo about the manner in which we creatively express who we are, and Sagittarius the way we go about finding a deeper, truer meaning for ourselves. All fire signs are about us—

they are personal. They have to do with the inner spirit and the need for action, movement, and change; they link with intuition and gut feelings.

Fire signs do things because they feel right. They take risks, rise to challenges, and confront trouble head-on because they have the drive to be themselves and show the world who they are. Aries, Leo, and Sagittarius are imbued with the glow of an inner fire that constantly propels them onward in order to live the most personally fulfilled and self-motivated life they can.

Fire signs are all highly individual, and when Saturn is in a fire sign, it hampers the individual from being who they truly are. When we realise that Saturn dampens down and restricts, it's easy to see that Saturn in Aries will affect an individual's renowned sense of self (Aries is the "me" sign) to the extent they feel unable to push themselves forward as they should. That bold, fast, naïve faith in the ability to tackle life head-on is seriously compromised when Saturn is in this sign. Individuals are more fearful of confrontation and less likely to take risks.

In Leo, Saturn will impede the natural expression of an individual's creativity. Leo is the sign of the actor, the showman, and the spokesperson, so it's easy to see how Saturn might undermine their innate self-confidence. Saturn in Leo may long to perform in public but lack the confidence to do so.

In Sagittarius, Saturn will make individuals wary of investigating a deeper meaning to life. Sagittarius rules the 9th house of individual thinking. It's the sign that wants to know "the truth," and this truth involves a constant search of ideas and theories. When Saturn is here, individuals will wonder why they can't seem to think outside the box when they know there must be so much more esoteric knowledge and universal truth waiting to be found. Instead, they will tend to cling to the ideas of others, because it saves them the discomfort and fear of thinking for themselves.

When Saturn is in a fire sign, it makes the individual very self-aware and conscious of their shortcomings, which is normally an alien concept to the fire signs, who live a life that is all about them. Saturn is a fear area, so despite very much wanting to be whole and confident, they have an intrinsic fear they aren't good enough. Sometimes it comes across as an exaggerated sense of self-importance, which is simply a cover for insecurity and the inability to be naturally spontaneous; this is especially so in the sign of Leo.

Saturn in the Earth Signs:
Taurus, Virgo, and Capricorn

The earth signs focus on material comfort and security. They are concerned about the tangible, real world and strive to create something they can touch, use, and benefit from. Earth signs are often given bad press because, in spiritual terms, striving for material comforts is seen as a lowly aim. In reality, the whole world is based on money, achievement, status, and the subsequent rewards. There is not one among us who doesn't consider our material welfare, who doesn't seek creature comforts; we all need to feel safe and secure, and we strive to make it so through an occupation, an income, a partner (generally), and a home. We make ourselves as comfortable and safe as possible. So, when Saturn is in an earth sign, it hampers the ability to find that security we all crave.

The sign of Taurus rules the 2nd house, which indicates how people feel about money and the way they go about acquiring it. Saturn in Taurus creates real issues with money and property; these issues can be almost soul-destroying. No matter what an individual does or how hard they work, Saturn will block their access to material things, either completely or until later in life, when it hardly seems to matter anymore. This is an extremely difficult placement, and my new theory will explain why someone may have Saturn in Taurus.

Those with Saturn in Virgo will have difficulty finding fulfilling work and may subsequently suffer health or mental problems. Virgo rules the 6th house of hands-on work and service, and when someone is prevented from expressing themselves in this way, their focus turns inward and causes psychological problems.

Capricorn has Saturn as its ruler. Thus, it is naturally hard-working, focussed, and materially minded. This is the one and only sign Saturn is comfortable in, but even so, as any Capricorn will attest to, life is tough. Individuals will make lifelong efforts to achieve dreamed-of rewards. Nothing comes easy with Saturn, not even when in its own sign—even here, Saturn delays rewards until old age.

Saturn in the Air Signs: Gemini, Libra, and Aquarius

The three air signs deal with the logical mind and thought processes, and they are detached and unemotional. Air signs express the need to connect with (or at least relate to) our fellow man. Gemini wants information and is the link between people, Libra wants justice and fairness, and Aquarius seeks an egalitarian society where humanitarian values are paramount. Saturn in these signs will restrict the free expression of ideas—the very role these three signs were designed for. When Saturn is in the picture, it is not only movement *but thought itself* that is impeded.

Gemini will feel Saturn's impediment the most, being the lightest, freest, and flightiest of the air signs. Geminis are the communicators of the zodiac, so either their communications will be hindered altogether or there will be a less diverse outlook, making conversations more focussed, worthy, and meaningful. If we think of the typical Gemini as a flippant comedian, it's easy to see how Saturn's restrictive nature will dampen their natural self-expression and lightness of heart.

The Libra who oversees those scales of justice will be inclined to be more judgemental and harsh, certainly a lot less lenient, when Saturn is in their sign. Saturn is viewed as the wise old teacher, so it can certainly bring benefits, but Saturn judges from an entirely different viewpoint than Libra, who is more fair. Saturn likes traditions, rules, and regulations, so judgements made may be harsher and come from a more severe baseline.

Aquarius is the sign of friendship. Generally, Aquarians have many friends from all walks of life and are the least judgemental sign of the zodiac, along with Pisces. Instead of an individual mindset, Aquarians have more of a group consciousness. Saturn disrupts that easy communication with others that they normally have, and it makes them more selective of who they mix with. Easygoing friendships will be more difficult to achieve, creating a feeling of personal isolation and loneliness.

Saturn in the Water Signs: Cancer, Scorpio, and Pisces

As we've seen, the fire signs take action and initiate change, the earth signs consolidate, and the air signs think and communicate. It is the water signs who feel.

Cancer is the most hands-on of the water signs. Cancer's role is to relate to others; they are the one who understands, the one who cares. Whether they offer a sympathetic listening ear or hands-on nursing, Cancer helps in whatever way they can. Saturn in Cancer will stop this flow of nurturance, and there is a reason for this, which we will discuss in chapter 3.

Equally as sensitive is Scorpio. Because of the intensity of Scorpio's emotions, they use self-defence to hide their vulnerability. This results in psychological interplays between themselves and others, all in an attempt to avoid being hurt. Along with all the usual undercurrents that are so prevalent in Scorpio's psyche, Saturn in this sign adds even more problems. The truth is, Saturn in Scorpio gets very bad press; some of these undercurrents aren't very nice at all. When we remember that Scorpio rules the 8th house of other people's money, death, sex, and psychology, it's easy to see the probable difficulties. How a Saturn in Scorpio will handle themselves all depends on how evolved the individual is.

Pisces, the mutable water sign, is a hotchpotch of conflicting yet sensitive emotions, which often take them over. They are subject to vague yet unexplained fears, usually over something that may happen in some distant future, and Saturn adds even more fear. When Saturn is in Pisces, it may rob individuals of any control they have over life. Saturn insists these individuals let go of what little ego they have, and it is the fear of being totally at the mercy of others' kindnesses—or not—that is their own personal nightmare.

three
Saturn Through the Signs and Houses

This chapter provides a detailed description of Saturn in all of the houses and signs. Check your birth chart to find out where your own Saturn is, by house and by astrological sign. Sometimes Saturn is very close to the cusp (start) of another house, so make sure to verify which house it is in by looking at the chart's list of planets. Even if Saturn is extremely close to the next house, the house it actually occupies is the one to use.

My aim in this chapter is to concentrate on how Saturn is felt in each house and sign and, based on my new no-go theory, what it is really saying about life direction. At the end of each section, there are real-life chart examples of people who have this Saturn placement. My intention is to make it as simple as possible to grasp Saturn's message, so whole charts won't be analysed; we will only be looking at the parts that are relevant. These examples illustrate how looking at the chart's sun sign and house, north node position, and area of emphasis will clarify what Saturn is saying about the individual's cosmic purpose.

Here is a brief guide to the quadrants: Not only are there top and bottom halves of a chart (above and below the horizon line), there are left and right halves. The left side is known as the "Me" side, and planets there are used for the individual—they are not worldly. The exception to this is any planet in the 12th house, for whom selfless service is a personal need or spiritual requirement (more on that later). The right side of the chart is the "Others" side, and planets here are used with and for others. In other words, the focus is on others rather than the self. The quadrants will become clearer as you work through your own Saturn position and the relevant examples. For a more detailed explanation of the quadrants, check out the appendix at the back of the book.

As you will see, Saturn's message is often very clear. Finding your true cosmic direction is often simpler than you'd think. I recommend first reading the section on the house that your Saturn occupies. Then, flip to the section that represents the sign your Saturn is in and read the provided example to gain further clarity. By drawing on the two, a clear picture of the area of life you are being asked to avoid (the house) and the manner in which you should go about it (the sign) will become clear. When you understand your own chart, have a go at interpreting Saturn's message in the charts of your partner, family members, and friends. That way, you'll gradually build up an understanding of how Saturn works and how to interpret its message.

Obviously, birth charts are multifaceted and contain a lot of other information. In some cases, it is necessary to include other aspects of a chart. If an individual's life purpose isn't completely clear from the three aspects itemised (sun, north nodes, quadrant), it is always advisable to look at the rest of the chart. In these cases, my advice is to take a look at the planet that rules the house Saturn is in. There is a list of house rulers in the appendix at the back of the book. For example, if Saturn is in the 3rd house, which is ruled by Mercury, have a look at where Mercury is in the chart to shed some light on life direction.

Note: There are real-life chart examples in this chapter. To ensure anonymity, I have changed people's names and omitted birth chart data in the following examples, with the exception of members of the British royal family, as this information is freely available online.

Saturn in the 1st House and/or Aries

The 1st house, known these days as the rising sign and to previous generations as the ascendant, is all about how we present ourselves to the world. It represents how we want others to see us. My belief—explored in detail in my previous book, *Secrets of Your Rising Sign*—is that an individual's rising sign was their sun sign in the previous life, which explains why we strongly resonate with the characteristics of the rising sign from the moment we are old enough to be self-aware. The rising sign provides us with a baseline until we gradually adapt to our new chart and new sun sign, which is there to guide and help us achieve our life purpose in this incarnation.

Aries rules the 1st house. It is the child in astrological terms; it is spring, the new baby, the new beginning. All beginnings need tremendous drive and force, firstly to be born, then to survive. Both this 1st house and its ruler, Aries, are about "me." This is the most personal sign and house. Everything we say and do gets filtered through the 1st house. It's how we act and how we like to be perceived, but it's also about our drive to be recognised as an individual. This house pushes us to grow and expand and survive using our own unique talents and abilities. It's the doorway to the self.

Knowing how important this 1st house is, imagine having Saturn here, blocking the ability to be who we truly are by making us afraid of stepping forward. Saturn suppresses whatever area it occupies.

If you have Saturn in the 1st house or in the sign of Aries, it is going to significantly impact your life in the most personal way. As I've shared, to survive requires a strong life force, but Saturn here will make you fearful of confrontation or standing up for what you believe in. It makes you timid, whereas Aries is usually bold. Mars, the ruler of Aries, is careless, aggressive, and driven. But the characteristics of Saturn are caution, reserve, conservatism, and authority. Saturn sits on Mars's life force when in this house and sign, making normally bold, brave Mars fearful and wary.

Regardless of what astrological sign is in your 1st house, Saturn in the rising sign will provide you with a natural reserve, dignity, and conservatism in thought and manner. It will also imbue you with the desire to avoid drawing attention to yourself and to avoid doing anything illegal or morally wrong. Remember, Saturn is the ruler of Capricorn, so it gives a tinge of Capricorn to your outward personality, and Capricorn is both traditional and highly moral.

The real negatives of this placement have to do with fear. Saturn creates fear, but Aries are not generally fearful souls, so to see a timid Aries is quite sad. Saturn here will make you think twice, question what you do, and fear confrontation—and standing up for yourself. You will feel as though you don't have any right to your opinion or your place in the world. Instead of showing yourself through your rising sign, you hide behind it, trying to avoid being noticed.

Previous astrological advice on how to handle this Saturn placement was to fight this shyness tooth and nail. This involved much psychological dwelling—not exactly an Aries forte. Quite frankly, most Aries feel they have far better things to do in life than spend it in self-introspection!

Spiritual Message of Saturn in the 1st House and/or Aries

Saturn is placed here for a valid reason, and in this house and sign it is saying something significant about your life path. Its message is: *I am here to remind you you're not supposed to be pushing yourself forward. This life is not about your own abilities and talents, but about being of service to others.*

If Saturn is in the 1st house and/or Aries, this lifetime is not about you. In fact, rather than hindering you, Saturn is here to *help*. Instead of fighting against your fears, step back and analyse the rest of your chart for two takeaways: first, why you are not supposed to pursue your own talents and abilities in this life, and second, what the real purpose of your life is.

Most charts with Saturn in the 1st house or in the sign of Aries are caring charts. An incredible number have the sun in the 6th house of service. The north nodes are often in a caring house/sign too, or at the bottom of the chart. The north nodes indicate the area of life that is not on display.

If you have this placement, my theory is that prior to this life, you made a conscious choice to repay karmic debts to others, or to give back to humanity in some way. That means that many of your own personal wishes and desires will not be achieved in this life. If you stop and think about it, you may realise that most of your life you've been trying hard but not getting very far, even though you are intelligent or gifted in some way. You may have felt incredibly frustrated at your lack of progress when other, seemingly less-gifted people sailed past you and achieved so much more! You might also feel frustrated by your lack of self-confidence and inner fears. These fears prevent you from achieving all you feel you could, if only you were bolder and braver.

But your life this time is not about material gain or being recognised for your own talents. It's about what you can do in service of mankind. In karmic/cosmic terms, you are earning brownie points and making huge strides in your spiritual development. It also suggests that you are a wise, older soul who made this conscious choice in order to progress spiritually; previous lifetimes have already been spent developing your own talents, so to do so again in this life is counterproductive.

Some say acceptance is the highest spiritual lesson, and it will certainly help to keep this in mind because once you let go and allow life to guide you rather than trying to mould it to your own desires, your life will become so much easier. Instead of constantly battling to be what you're not and trying to advance against all odds, you can step back and see your chart's message in its true light.

So, what is your path and destiny? To discover your soul path in this life, check:

1. Your sun's house and sign
2. What the north nodes are saying about your life direction
3. The quadrant emphasis ("Me," "Others," collective, or individual thinking)

Once the light of understanding has illuminated your path, be kind to yourself instead of feeling frustrated and blocked, because yours is a truly spiritual path.

Example: Saturn in the 1st House (In Leo)

We only have to look to the current Queen of England, Camilla Parker-Bowles, to see Saturn in the 1st house in action. Queen Camilla also has:

- Sun in the 12th house in Cancer
- North nodes in the 11th house (south nodes in the 5th house)
- Me-sided chart emphasis

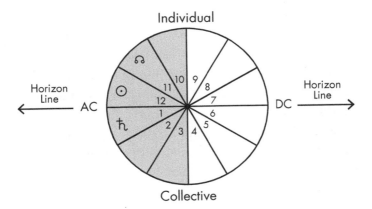

Saturn sits just below Camilla's ascendant in the 1st house, a sure indicator that her life isn't about her, but is meant to be lived for others. In the sign of Leo, too, she will be unable to express her own personal talents. (See the section on Saturn in Leo on page 72.)

Camilla also has most of her important personal planets tucked away in the 12th house; the sun, moon, Mercury, and Venus are all in this house, a place not visible to the outside world. Thus, she personally feels the energy of these planets but observers aren't able to access her via them, as 12th house planets are used solely by the individual. What this means is she has a highly spiritual dimension to her chart, and coupled with Saturn in the 1st, it is clear that all her outward actions (those seen by the world) should be for the benefit of others.

Camilla's chart emphasis is on the Me side of the chart. In her last life, she lived in the 5th house (her south nodes are here), which is on the Others side of the chart. This means she would have mixed with people from all walks of life. In fact, she brought this feeling over with her into this life—she was renowned as a party girl in her youth. Camilla felt comfortable in pubs, clubs, and bars, having fun, enjoying herself, and mixing with anyone and everyone. But she could not stay here because in this life, her north nodes are in the 11th house of selective friendship groups. Camilla's task was to learn to be more selective of whom she mixed with and to live amongst a select group, which is exactly what has happened.

With her north nodes in the 11th (and especially with those important personal planets in the 12th, plus Saturn in the 1st and in Leo), Queen Camilla has been guided to a humanitarian life where the good of others comes before her own personal comfort. She can take what she knows of the 5th house and the lessons she learnt there, which have given her a natural ease when dealing with people, and use this ability in her humanitarian and charitable work.

Me-sided charts are those that do not interact in a personal way with others. Their task is a personal search for meaning and purpose. Thus, the queen's forays into the world may be in the public eye, but she is not putting her own talents and personality on display. Instead, she is merely being a figurehead for what many British people consider an important historical institution. As someone who was not born into royalty, nor who expected to become a queen, we can only surmise (based on her chart information) that it might be hard for Camilla to sacrifice her own needs, desires, and wishes in order to play a more public role.

King Charles is a Scorpio sun, moon in Taurus character, both of which are fixed, stubborn signs. This explains his steely determination not be thwarted when he aimed to have this lady as his wife. His Taurus moon, particularly, indicates that once he made up his mind it was Camilla he wanted, he would leave no stone unturned to have her—which is exactly what happened.

And so we see this lady's chart in action. Camilla finally accepted the yoke and bowed to the greater good, giving up her personal freedom in all senses, both figuratively and literally. Queen Camilla followed the direction her chart was leading her, but she did so later in life, which is often the case with the north nodes. We approach them gradually, in small steps. Camilla's reward is having Jupiter in the 4th house. She is blessed with abundant and comfortable homes and a luxurious lifestyle as a reward for her sacrifices.

Many people assume being royal is a gift, but when undertaken with a sense of serious duty, it is anything but. Camilla's cosmic path was set at her birth, and she must have known for years that one day she would be required to undertake her spiritual destiny and let go of the personal for the greater good. Saturn's message is quite clear.

To sum up, in her last life, Camilla was out in the world mixing with all sorts of people. With her south node below the horizon line, especially being in the 5th house, she would have lived amongst these people in a rough-and-ready fashion. Her Saturn is in Leo, so she might have been an actor or used her artistic abilities in some way. Either way, she was part of the collective at the bottom of the chart. But in this life, Camilla's task is to do the opposite, and nothing is as removed from the busy collective as the 11th house of royalty (an extremely select group). This lifetime isn't about her own talents at all, but about serving others while at the same time finding her own spiritual path (sun in the 12th) via selfless service.

Example: Saturn in Aries (In the 10th House)

Pam is in her mid-eighties, but she is very active and alert. For most of her life, she worked in private medical facilities on the administration side. She married once, after her retirement. Pam has:

- Sun in the 6th house in Capricorn
- North nodes in the 4th house (south nodes in the 10th house)
- Collective area emphasis

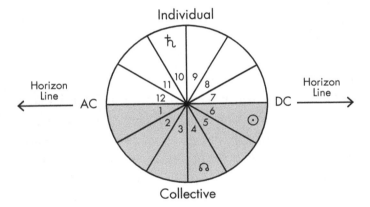

Pam's Saturn in Aries is saying that her own wishes and desires are not the point of this life—service to others is. Her sun in the 6th house also confirms she should use her energy in the service of others. The sun is below the AC/DC line, so this service will not be on public display in this lifetime.

A life of service does not literally mean toiling for others; it means a conscious decision to be supportive of others and helpful to them. Being below the AC/DC line does not make one's life less important. In fact, often the opposite is true. Much is achieved behind the scenes, and for the most part, it is highly significant. It's like the phrase "the power behind the throne." There is always a spiritual aspect to service to others, because when we think of others rather than ourselves, we access a more spiritually evolved part of ourselves.

Pam's collective area emphasis shows she should spend her life at the bottom of the chart, keeping busy within her community, which is exactly what she did. Even now, at eighty-five, she runs her local church almost single-handedly, organising and planning and standing centre stage when required. She finds great joy in her role and is appreciated and admired by all who know her.

Pam's Saturn in the 10th shows her no-go area (see page 112 for more information on Saturn in the 10th house). A high-flying career is not something Pam could ever have achieved because of her 4th house north nodes/10th house south nodes, which confirm she had a high-profile career in her last life that gave her status and recognition. In this lifetime, Pam has to be content with her home and family; she has to learn to accept the invisibility that comes with unsung caring.

The message of Pam's placements is that in her last life, she was a career person with a very high profile. She was probably famous or well-known. In this life, she is balancing that by doing the opposite: learning to stay below the horizon line and to serve others and her community. It is Saturn's position that shows us exactly what she should stay away from in this life.

By analysing these aspects of Pam's chart—all of which reinforce the same message—it is obvious that Pam's life was meant to be one of service and not one in which she could make her own wishes and dreams felt. While Pam may not have known the spiritual purpose behind the things that happened in her life, her chart clearly showed what she should *not* be doing.

Saturn in the 2nd House and/or Taurus

The 2nd house is usually described as what we own or seek to own. It's where astrologers assess how someone feels about money, acquisitions, and possessions. One thing that is often overlooked is that it also deals with our values. If we are going to work to own something, it must have value for us. So, in truth, the 2nd house is more about what we value, with the owning of that desired possession the result. Both the sign of Taurus and the house it rules take pleasure from ownership. Because Taurus is a fixed earth sign, the focus is on the tangible things in life which, once owned, cannot be taken away.

Nothing about life is safe or predictable. Houses can be devalued through the vagaries of economic fluctuations, jobs can be lost, and the people we love can most certainly leave. But Taurus, more than any other sign, endeavours to make it so.

Individuals with Saturn in Taurus and/or the 2nd house likely had a particularly difficult time growing up. They would have become aware that money was an issue in their family. Because money is such an emotive issue, by the time these children reached school age, they may have had an acute awareness of how little they had in relation to others. Now, in some way or another, money and what their family owns (or, more likely, doesn't own) will be something that these individuals carry with them into adulthood, with the knowledge that they don't want to continue living this way. As they age, they think that if they work very hard, they can achieve what their family didn't: a house, a nice car, money in the bank as a buffer against hard times, or even a secure relationship. When they were young, they probably witnessed arguments about money that involved accusations and complaints (after all, money is one of the primary reasons couples argue), and so they are conscious of wanting a harmonious, secure relationship. The 2nd house is ruled by the planet Venus, which desires a calm, peaceful life in every respect.

Money issues can also work in reverse. If an individual grew up in a household where there was a great deal of money and money was perceived as the *raison d'être*, this can also cause problems. It's likely they will have an overpowering need to cling to money and property but lack confidence in their ability to stand alone financially. So, even if their family was rich, those with a Saturn in Taurus and/or the 2nd house will struggle with financial issues. They are used to having everything, so how can they survive without the same level of comfort? They feel they do not have the tools their parents had to succeed. The bar has been set too high.

All children feel a need to be better than their parents —to do better, to have more—because that's what parents expect, even if it's a subliminal message: that their children will launch themselves from the platform they have created and take the baton forward. Overly high expectations can make children feel inadequate or cause them to overlook their own unique talents and abilities in the pursuit of making money, especially if their interests and abilities are completely different from their parents'.

For those of you with Saturn here, the natural desire to make yourself secure is beset by real fears regarding money and security. You go above and beyond in your need to acquire material wealth; it can become your be-all and end-all—an obsession. This is a natural result of having Saturn in Taurus and/or the 2nd house because you have subconscious knowledge that security will be denied in this life. This is the fear that Saturn is so good at creating, and in this case, the fear is well founded.

Saturn in the 2nd will also affect how you value yourself. If you place a low value on your ability to earn enough money to make yourself secure, you might look to others to do it for you. Not everyone is worldly, commercially minded, and comfortable in the real world, where we all buy and sell our skills in order to survive.

Spiritual Message of Saturn in the 2nd House and/or Taurus

Whatever your childhood was like, if you have Saturn in the 2nd house and/or Taurus, you will endure a life of hardship when it comes to money and property. You will probably earn enough to get by, but the security level you'd prefer is unattainable. Your focus on money will run like a thread throughout your life, yet it will be hard for you to make any real progress no matter how hard you try. Saturn's message is: *I am here to teach you how unimportant material wealth is when it comes to obtaining personal happiness.*

Those with Saturn in the 2nd house naturally look to the opposite house for a solution. The 2nd/8th house axis is called the money axis. The 2nd house represents your own money and property, whereas its opposite house, the 8th, represents other people's money and property. If you find yourself unable to earn enough money to make yourself se-cure—and this is the result of Saturn here, in the 2nd house and/or Taurus—you'll look to other people to provide what you lack. Perhaps this is your cosmic lesson: to learn to re-ceive, when in other lives you were accustomed to being the benefactor. In past lives, it's likely you were wealthy; you were too obsessed with the material over the spiritual.

To discover your soul path in this life, check:

1. Your sun's house and sign
2. What the north nodes are saying about your life direction
3. The quadrant emphasis ("Me," "Others," collec-tive, or individual thinking)

The house the sun occupies will show where to focus your drive in this life, and the north nodes often reinforce this in some way by showing you how to achieve personal happiness and fulfilment regardless of money. When Sat-urn is in the 2nd house and/or Taurus, your task is to ac-cept that life will be hard in financial terms, no matter how hard you strive to alter the situation. To gain inner peace and contentment, acceptance of this fact is neces-sary. Only then will you live a life that truly brings you happiness. Money is not the only way to achieve this; in fact, most people with money are no happier than anyone else. As we are often reminded, money cannot buy health or real love, which are the two things most of us want.

Example: Saturn in the 2nd House (In Sagittarius)

Jean is a middle-aged Romanian lady. Her Saturn is in the 2nd house. She also has:

- Sun in the 1st house in Scorpio
- North nodes in the 12th house (south nodes in the 6th house)
- Me-sided chart emphasis

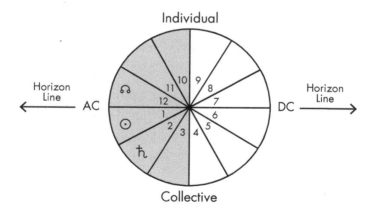

Jean's Saturn in the 2nd house indicates that this life will be difficult financially, with security via money and property elusive. When she was young, Jean lived in Romania. Few ordinary people had material wealth, so she was not alone in this. But because Jean had Saturn in the 2nd house, it galled her excessively. Later, as a young adult, Jean had the choice of two men to marry. The one she chose—who appeared to have better prospects at the time—did not succeed in life, and so Jean's own life was one of hardship in material terms.

Jean had two daughters whom she pressed to further their education in the hope that they would support her, but both chose a different path. Jean's daughters eventually separated from their mother due to her continual obsession with money and her desire to control them for her own benefit.

Because the astrological sign in Jean's 2nd house is Sagittarius (check out page 105 for more information on Saturn in the 9th/Sagittarius), it was impossible for her to try and force her children into her way of thinking. Jean's Saturn in Sagittarius indicates she cannot enforce her views on others, particularly those of an esoteric/religious nature. No matter how persuasive Jean was, she could not get her daughters—or anyone else—to see her point of view on most issues. Jean is strongly religious and follows the religion of her home country, which is Greek Orthodox. This adherence to the accepted religion is very indicative of Saturn in Sagittarius. This placement often refuses to see anything but the accepted religious path. Jean's insistence that her daughters follow her own belief system was another reason they chose to separate from their mother.

Jean has an extremely challenging chart. She has five planets in the 1st house, very close to the ascendant, one of which is her sun; all five planets are in Scorpio. Throughout her life, Jean has attempted to use the force of her personality to manipulate others. (Scorpio not only hides its true motives from others in this 1st house, but it is adept at manipulation—unless the individual is highly evolved spiritually.)

Because Jean's sun is in the 1st house, her rising sign, she was supposed to use the force of her personality at Scorpio's highest vibration. (See my book *Secrets of Your Rising Sign* to learn what having the sun in the 1st house means regarding cosmic life lessons.) However, that was not the case. Scorpio can be a manipulative, controlling sign, and because Jean used the negative energy of this position, she pushed away the people she cared about most in her quest for financial security.

Additionally, Jean's chart indicates that she was not supposed to follow an established religion at all. With her north nodes in the 12th house, she is being guided to find spiritual peace through contemplation and isolation. Saturn in the 2nd is denying her material wealth so that she is forced to confront the things that really matter in life, and in Sagittarius, she is being warned not to follow any particular religion or creed (nor should she impress these beliefs on others). If Jean followed her birth chart's directives, she would feel her way to her own private spiritual beliefs.

Now, Jean is alone, which is indicative of the north nodes in the 12th house. And, with her quadrant emphasis on the left side of her chart, this is where she should be. In the coming years, hopefully Jean will be able to find some inner peace and contentment and come to terms with her extremely difficult life.

It is interesting that Jean's chart is what I call "tight." There was little room for manoeuvring. My assumption is that in previous lives, she failed to reach her 12th house, so she was given little chance to make an error this time. Jean's whole life path is heading towards the 12th house. Regardless of what she does, she cannot escape her destiny.

Example: Saturn in Taurus (In the 5th House)

This must be the clearest chart I've ever interpreted. Donna is in her mid-thirties. She is vivacious and enjoys the party life—she never says no if she is asked to go out. Her Saturn is in Taurus. Donna also has:

- Sun in the 4th house in Aries
- North nodes in the 7th house (south nodes the 1st house)
- Others-sided chart emphasis

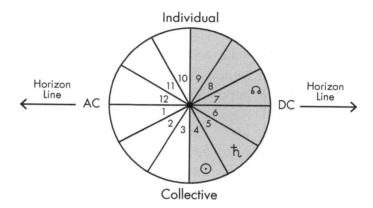

Donna is very independent and confident, which is unsurprising with her south node in Capricorn in the 1st house. Capricorn is the career sign, so it's likely she had a high profile career in the last life. And, since her south node is in the 1st house, Donna is accustomed to doing things her way, without taking others into account.

Donna's Saturn in Taurus indicates that this life will be hard in financial terms. Although she has no problem attracting partners, Donna tends to pick unreliable men, a few of whom have fleeced her of what little money she has.

She lives in a small flat in a very poor area of town, and despite working long hours in a supermarket, she hardly makes ends meet.

Donna tells me she would like to settle down because then she might have some security, but she finds it hard to compromise and adjust to partners, which is why she prefers to keep things light. Once, Donna was briefly married, but her husband left, citing her inability to be faithful. This is her past-life independence in action (south node in the 1st house).

Donna's Saturn in the 5th house indicates that this life is not about expressing her unique talents. The 5th house is also the place of random love affairs, which are being given the thumbs down with Saturn here.

With her north nodes in the seventh house, it is quite clear that this life is meant to be a learning one regarding partnerships. Donna's task is learning to balance her own needs with those of a long-term partner; she must learn how to share and compromise. Her north nodes are in the sign of Cancer, so Donna is learning how to move from independent, capable Capricorn to the hands-on care of Cancer. This is further emphasised by her sun being in the 4th house of home and family, another clear message of where to focus her energies.

It appears that in her last life, Donna proved she could manage just fine on her own and financially supported herself. In this life, Donna is clearly being shown her cosmic path: Her Saturn is in Taurus (preventing financial gain) in the 5th house (preventing random love affairs and the expression of her unique talents); her sun is in the 4th house (showing her she should focus her energies on family life); her north nodes are in the 7th house (showing her path in this life is a long-term, committed relationship), *and* she has an Others chart emphasis (explaining that other people are the focus of this life, not herself). This is almost a complete reversal of Donna's past life, which is why she struggles to adapt. Saturn is forcing Donna to depend on others, as this is the 2nd/8th house axis in action: If we can't gain money by our own efforts, we need to look to others to help us.

Donna is now realising that she doesn't want to be independent forever and is currently dating a man who seems to like her a lot. We can only wish her luck and hope that now that she understands her chart, Donna may make more of an effort to allow her relationship to grow.

Saturn in the 3rd House and/or Gemini

Gemini is an air sign, and all air signs are difficult to pin down. Gemini, the messenger of the zodiac with the role of passing on information, finds it hard to settle for any one idea, job, person, or lifestyle. Geminis are the link between people. Although they are often thought of as superficial, they have an important role in life, and none more so than during the recent pandemic. It was the Geminis who opened up new methods of communication when physical meetings became impossible.

The 3rd house, ruled by Gemini, is in the collective area of the chart, at the bottom. The 3rd house deals with education, though the education here is generally considered the sort taught by rote up to the age of eighteen—the age when we start to think for ourselves. As children, we learn how to behave, how to communicate, and what to believe while in the 3rd house of education. Aside from the influence of home and family, the 3rd house is where human socialisation happens. In effect, the 3rd house is essentially our whole world while growing up, as it encompasses neighbours, siblings, and friends; short journeys in the local area; and communication of all sorts, including the general, friendly, gossipy information that passes between people on a daily basis.

Gemini is often perceived as a shallow sign because of its intellectual flitting here and there, but Gemini's forte is words; many of our greatest comedians are Geminis. They can also be found in newspaper and magazine journalism, on television and the radio, in the midst of celebrity culture and fashion, and in many of the numerous and varied forms of daily communication. This sign is ruled by the planet Mercury, named after the winged messenger of Roman mythology (and Hermes in Greek mythology), so Geminis have a vital role in keeping the human race in touch with each other.

Geminis rarely have the intellectual stamina to write a novel or do any sort of research, not because they can't but because they usually lose interest (unless earthy placements ground them). This is a light-hearted, take-nothing-seriously sign, and Geminis are renowned for constantly changing their mind. But that's only because they see all possibilities, and all are doable! How can they possibly decide the best route to take when all look interesting? For Geminis, there is no right or wrong. Because they do not invest emotion in their words or in ideas, they leave themselves free to explore in a non-judgemental way. Gemini's role is to pass on information and link people to each other—they aren't meant to judge an idea, just to convey it.

The real message of the 3rd house is that as social beings, we need to connect, and it is through these daily interactions that we function as a society. Social media blossomed during lockdown because people felt so isolated we opened up new avenues of communication, which shows how important it is to us as a species. This is Gemini in action, doing what it is meant to do: keep us connected.

If you have Saturn in the 3rd house and/or Gemini, this flow of ideas, this natural communication that occurs between us all, is blocked on a basic level. You can—and do—connect with others, but it is often through intellectual groups or scientific studies. You have a serious mindset, which is alien to the sign of Gemini; you find it hard to make light chitchat. You likely have difficulty expressing your own personal needs and desires. Sometimes this extends to other areas, like keeping in touch with people; you may even have a problem learning languages. This does not by any means imply a lack of intelligence—often, quite the opposite is true.

Psychologists believe problems start in childhood, so they would have a field day blaming your upbringing or your family for stifling your natural expression as a child. Perhaps your parents were too strict, religiously intolerant, or not interested in hearing your opinion, a sort of modern day seen-but-not-heard scenario, which hampered your freedom of expression. But if we look at it logically, Saturn was here the moment you were born, so it is a fated position. This presupposes a prior spiritual arrangement—you were destined to have this type of restriction. But why? What is Saturn saying?

If Saturn is in the 3rd house and/or Gemini, you are certainly being asked to look deeper into subjects and to avoid unnecessary conversations. It is likely you are quiet, sometimes monosyllabic, when general conversation is held around you, probably because the conversation is of no interest to you. Maybe it seems too frivolous? Saturn here indicates an academic/researcher mindset, so you are only motivated to converse with those who have something important to say. Enjoyment comes from deep and meaningful conversations, which is totally unlike this sign and house when Saturn isn't here.

There is an important reason for every Saturn placement, and yours will be reinforced by the rest of your chart. Perhaps, in past lives, you concentrated on the frivolous, gossipy aspects of life, and this time there is a higher cosmic aim for you. Maybe you need to spend your time searching for the answers to scientific, medical, or engineering problems, or to study esoteric subjects. This placement may be asking you to devote yourself to deep investigation into your chosen subject.

Spiritual Message of Saturn in the 3rd House and/or Gemini

This Saturn placement suggests too many lifetimes have been spent in idle chitchat. It is now time to start stretching your mind. To encourage this predetermined life path, Saturn has blocked all connection to anything that isn't of a serious nature. When you try to build a fan base on YouTube or get thousands of hits on your website or blog, it will fail, regardless of how clever or entrepreneurial you are. However, be aware that this social media blockage only applies when dealing with general conversation. If you choose serious, worthy subjects that you have studied in depth, you will be accessing the 9th house, which is an area you will be able to freely use; many people with a block in the 3rd do have helpful planets in the 9th. In this case, the information you share must come from your own research and your own theories and not just rehash others' ideas. Only then will you be able to use your 9th house effectively.

The old advice of trying to overcome Saturn's limitations and access the 3rd house's ease of communication is exactly what you *aren't* supposed to be doing. Instead, you should take Saturn's advice and avoid the area altogether. When Saturn is in the 3rd house and/or Gemini, its message is: *You have a higher path to follow and must avoid becoming involved in less-meaningful communications in the collective area of the chart.*

So, what is your path and destiny? To discover your soul path in this life, check:

1. Your sun's house and sign
2. What the north nodes are saying about your life direction
3. The quadrant emphasis ("Me," "Others," collective, or individual thinking)

By analysing the sun's house and sign and the north/south nodes, your life's purpose will become clear.

Example: Saturn in the 3rd House (In Libra)

Sue was one of my students, and an extremely gifted one. She is a quick and able learner, with a huge curiosity about everything esoteric. Sue's Saturn is in the 3rd house. She also has:

- Sun in the 9th house in Aries
- North nodes in the 12th house (south nodes in the 6th house)
- Individual thinking area emphasis

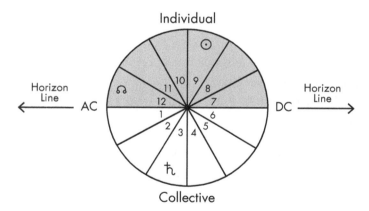

Sue's Saturn in the 3rd house indicates she mustn't indulge in gossip and chitchat and should instead look to higher subjects.

For a while now, Sue has desired to start her own business. But all her efforts with Instagram, Facebook, YouTube, and her own website have failed to succeed in the way she would have liked. This is frustrating for her, as she sees other, less-gifted people achieve worldly success while she does not. The reason Sue is unable to be successful is because social media is an aspect of the 3rd house, and there sits her Saturn, saying *no*.

So, what should Sue be doing instead? With her sun (and Mercury) in the independent sign of Aries in the 9th house, this is a sure sign of her life direction. Sue is very self-motivated and driven to keep learning, to keep digging for truths (Sagittarius rules the 9th house, and it seeks the true answers), and to keep pushing the boundaries of her knowledge. But this knowledge is for her alone (Aries is the "me" sign), and this is why she is blocked from the 3rd house: This learning is meant to be personal, not to be shared.

But *why* is Saturn there? Well, look at Sue's north node. It's in the 12th house. In her last life (or lives), Sue worked hard in the 6th house of serving others. This time, life is about her own intellectual and spiritual advancement via the 9th house, with the aim of reaching the 12th house. Neither of these houses are social areas; the 9th is private, personal study, and the 12th is the area we go to contemplate and meditate on our purpose, from which we form our spiritual beliefs.

Interestingly, Sue also has an all-red efficiency triangle with its apex on the north nodes in the 12th house, showing her, once again, that this is the area she should direct her energy. (See the appendix to learn more about this aspect pattern.)

Sue's Saturn in the sign of Libra indicates she must not allow partnerships to be the be-all and end-all of her life, because they will draw her away from her cosmic path. Saturn in Libra does not deny anyone relationships—it merely advises that we shouldn't invest all of our time and attention on them, usually because we have a higher path to follow. When Saturn is in Libra, it is common for individuals to have a more detached, cooler partnership. Although married, Sue and her husband have grown apart; while they live together, they act independently.

Learning the information provided in her birth chart gave Sue an understanding of why she kept getting blocked. Now, in order to fulfil her cosmic destiny in this lifetime, Sue can concentrate her energy where she is meant to: on personal, private esoteric studies (9th house), which will lead her to her 12th house north nodes and discovering her spiritual purpose and beliefs.

Example: Saturn in Gemini (In the 10th House)

Lorna is in her early fifties and comes from Europe. Her Saturn is in Gemini. She also has:

- Sun in the 7th house in Pisces
- North node in the 5th in Capricorn (south nodes in the 11th house)
- Others-sided chart emphasis

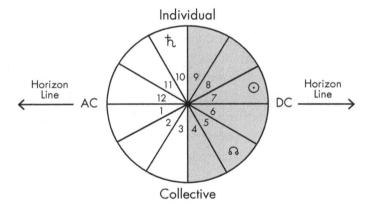

Lorna's chart is interesting as both her relationship houses, the 7th and the 5th, are prominent—most of her personal planets are there. As she has an Others quadrant emphasis, it's clear where Lorna's energy should be focussed in this life: on others and on her relationships.

Lorna's Saturn in Gemini indicates gossip and social media are areas she cannot access.

Lorna emigrated to the United Kingdom and struggled to learn English, so she had extra tutoring. This is very indicative of one possible problem when Saturn is in Gemini: a difficulty with language. This example shows the myriad ways a Saturn placement can impact someone's life.

Saturn is in the 10th house, which indicates a high-profile career is not Lorna's cosmic path in this life, especially one that involves communication. However, Lorna's chart does indicate a career of some kind; her north nodes are in the 5th house in Capricorn (Capricorn rules the career area). The north nodes are guiding her to use her creative talents (the 5th house is ruled by Leo and is about creative self-expression), not her communication skills (Gemini) in her career.

In fact, Lorna is already using her 5th house north nodes and Mars placements to be creative in both her artwork (she has had her work displayed in churches) and the small cookery business she runs. These north nodes also advise her to be less judgemental about people; her south node comfort zone is the 11th house of selective friendship. In her last life, it's likely Lorna was a career person with a selective group of friends who used a form of communication in her career. In this life, Lorna is being blocked from a career via the 10th house—she is being forced to follow her north node path in the 5th.

Lorna's jobs will put her in contact with all sorts of people from all walks of life (5th house). She has been given understanding personal planets (in Pisces in the 7th, the marriage/long-term relationship house) to make sure she learns her cosmic lessons of being compassionate and accepting of all. And, with the sign of Capricorn as her 5th house north nodes sign, it is clear that her career focus should be in the collective area of the chart.

While Lorna has yet to find her long-term partner, she is on the right track with her career, so life will present her with someone at the right time. This is a given, especially with three important planets in the 7th house, including her sun.

Saturn in the 4th House and/or Cancer

The 4th house is ruled by Cancer, which is a water sign that seeks to make everyone family. They care for, nurture, and heal others. This is a very sensitive area of the chart. The 4th house represents our roots, our family. Nothing touches us so deeply, so emotionally, as the family we grew up in. As children, we are rarely allowed glimpses into other families' more private moments, so it was our family of origin that taught us how to behave in the privacy of the home. Arguments, discussions, the ways we enjoyed ourselves, the settling of disputes—everything about how we act and think is based on what we learned at home and how our parents behaved in all circumstances. Whether we meant to or not, we watched how our parents acted and often used them as role models. Family life is fundamental in how we relate to others later in life, especially romantic partners.

When Saturn is in the 4th house, there was usually some kind of difficulty during childhood. It could be abuse of some kind, or even a coldness (real or perceived) that affected the future and how we behave within our own family unit when we become parents ourselves. Saturn creates fear and coldness, and the 4th house is a difficult area to experience this, as it hits at the very core of who we are. If our parents can't love us, who else will? How can we form our own happy family when we have no idea how to go about it?

By no means does Saturn here imply a direct form of abuse, although it is a possibility. There are many scenarios that can make us feel unloved or unwanted, even when we were actually deeply loved. This could look like a parent (or parents) who worked long hours and was so tired they couldn't provide us with hugs and attention, a single parent who provided for us but had no energy left to listen to our problems or help us solve them, the death of a parent, frequent separation from a parent because they worked abroad or travelled often, or a parent who did not know how to relate to us while actually loving and providing for us. All are expressions of Saturn in Cancer and/or the 4th house.

If there was any kind of coldness or rejection, Cancer —being a deeply sensitive sign aware of even the slightest nuance—felt that hurt deeply. It seeped into the psyche's core and stays lodged there for life. It is inevitable that those with this placement will mistrust emotional intimacy, so it's highly likely attachments formed later in life will be slightly askew. Perhaps an individual's chosen partner had a similar childhood, so there is an understanding of each other's experiences; yet, deep down, neither can really provide the other with what they require, because nothing and no one can make up for what their childhood lacked.

While childhood was likely difficult, siblings may have had very different experiences. Because each of us has a different birth chart and, thus, a different path in life, we perceive the same situation differently. Some can shrug off an unsatisfactory home life and go on to have settled relationships; for others, it is impossible. Some cling to their birth family and the area they grew up in; others loathe their family and move far away from them. If an individual has a lot of trauma associated with childhood, they may even seek revenge by refusing to see their family or in some way repaying the pain they felt.

If you have Saturn in the 4th house and/or Cancer, you likely envy others who have what you perceive to be a happy home life. As a result, you may form relationships prematurely or without due consideration in order to make up for the dark hole within. You crave a secure home life so deeply that you often attempt to create it with someone unsuitable.

Those of you with Saturn in the 4th house quickly learn to develop a veneer of self-assurance and reliance. This attracts weaker people who may cling to you for support. Your first foray into a serious relationship may attract the wrong type of partner; there will be a prolonged and painful emotional struggle until you eventually separate yourself from this partner and find someone more balanced. Breakups take a long time because you resist inflicting hurt on someone who has already been hurt. But for you, feeling used but not loved will activate old emotions, and you'll feel trapped, unhappy, and unappreciated for who you really are.

Spiritual Message of Saturn in the 4th house and/or Cancer

If you have Saturn in the 4th house and/or Cancer, you likely had a difficult childhood. Saturn here implies that a happy family is not guaranteed. This placement sends a message: *In spiritual terms, a family is not your path in this lifetime.*

With that being said, this Saturn placement doesn't mean you have to live alone. It indicates that you must not dedicate your entire life to the resolution of your emotional problems and the formation of the perfect family. Almost all of us need company and companionship, as humans are sociable beings—Saturn is not denying you relationships. Rather, Saturn in the 4th house and/or Cancer indicates that this life is not primarily about family—your path is an entirely different one. And so, Saturn was placed here to show you where *not* to focus your energy.

In previous lifetimes, your family supported you so much that you came to rely too heavily on them. In this life, you are being given a more difficult childhood—and perhaps less sympathetic, though not necessarily unkind, parents—to force you away from home so you seek your independence. In this life, you cannot become too reliant on your family's support. It may be that you are destined to have a spiritual life, and your path requires you to do so without a supportive family as you rely only on your individual faith and courage.

It is likely that other aspects of your birth chart are strong, giving you the ability to find your way alone, or certainly without the full support of a family unit. There is a reason for every placement in a birth chart, so accepting this aspect will help you grow as an individual.

So, what is your path and destiny? To discover your soul path in this life, check:

1. Your sun's house and sign
2. What the north nodes are saying about your life direction
3. The quadrant emphasis ("Me," "Others," collective, or individual thinking)

By analysing the sun's house and sign, the north/south nodes, and your chart's quadrant emphasis, your life purpose and cosmic path will become clear. Other aspects of the chart can also guide you. For example, self-worth is usually found through a career (the 10th house of career being on the other end of this 4th/10th house axis).

Example: Saturn in the 4th House (In Virgo)

Ben is a middle-aged man and an only child. He has been married and divorced twice. His Saturn sits in his 4th house. He also has:

- Sun in the 10th house in Aquarius
- North nodes in the 4th house (south nodes in the 10th house)
- Individual thinking area emphasis

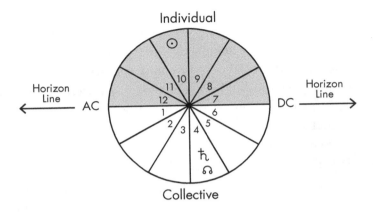

Ben admits that although his parents gave him everything he wanted, there was an emotional coolness in his household—his parents were not demonstrative. In some ways, he could cope with this, as three of his personal planets are in Aquarius, meaning he was slightly detached himself; he felt he was not a tactile person in a general way. But it is clear from his description of his two failed marriages that this lack of emotional closeness impaired his own ability to form a family. Ben's Saturn in the 4th house indicates a family is not his path in this life, and he should look to other areas of his chart for fulfilment.

At age thirty, Ben married and went on to have two children. After fifteen years, while still married to his first wife, Ben met another lady, fell in love with her, and set up home with her and her two children.

Both relationships failed.

Ben admits to knowing he should feel bad about leaving his first wife, but he doesn't. He says that although he fell in love with the second lady, he ended up having that same feeling of detachment from his new family as from his first. After a while, it dawned on Ben that he feels trapped and restricted by family life and the routine required.

Ben's north nodes are in the 4th house, right beside Saturn but not quite conjunct. Saturn in the same house as the north node is indicative of a *personal* search (in other words, a lot of inner, emotional searching) to come to terms with childhood coldness; yet, a family life is still to be avoided for spiritual reasons. Ben has many cosmic— possibly karmic—lessons to learn about the 4th house in this lifetime. It seems that whatever family Ben creates will result in the same feelings for him: being detached and unloved, no matter how hard his partners try to give him all he needs.

Ben's Saturn in Virgo indicates he worked hard behind the scenes in previous lives and is not supposed to be of service to others via the 4th house. This is not an area where he can roll up his sleeves and get involved, leaving his partners with the majority of the day-to-day house-hold tasks and childcare (which both wives complained about). Ben also suffers from all sorts of psychosomatic illnesses and fears of possible future illness, which is very indicative of Saturn in Virgo (or the 6th).

Basically, Ben is not supposed to be involved with the bottom of his chart, and family is at the bottom; his sun and the majority of his personal planets are at the top of his birth chart, as is his quadrant emphasis. If Ben had understood his chart decades ago, this could have saved both himself and his families from much heartache.

With his sun at the top of the chart in the 10th house, Ben is clearly being guided to a career in this life. Several personal planets in Aquarius show he is driven to do good for humanity, and his career choice reflects that. Certainly, Ben can have relationships, but he would be advised to avoid making commitments and spending all his energy on family; instead, he should concentrate his efforts on his career.

Ben's north nodes in the 4th house indicate that despite his upbringing, he will pursue the feeling of family throughout his life, and I suspect it will gradually unfold in relation to his children and step-children; when Saturn and the north nodes share a house, the learning curve regarding that house is a personal one. The position of Saturn will not change, but his way of perceiving and understanding his role in relation to his family unit will undergo many changes in this life until Ben realises this path is not the one that will bring him the most fulfilment.

Example: Saturn in Cancer (In the 8th House)

Nikki is in her early forties. She has had two failed marriages and a third failed long-term relationship. She works extremely hard and has a high-profile career. Her Saturn is in Cancer. Nikki also has:

- Sun in the 11th house in Libra
- North nodes in the 10th house (south nodes in the 4th house)
- Me-sided chart emphasis and individual thinking area emphasis

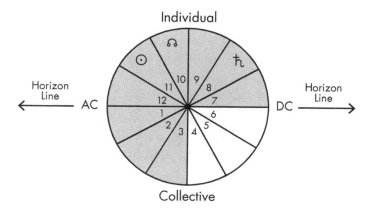

Nikki's Saturn in Cancer indicates a family life is to be avoided in this lifetime. However, because the 4th house of home and family is her south node comfort zone, Nikki did pursue a family; she had two children, even though almost all of her planets are in the upper left section of her birth chart and she has no planets in the 5th house of children.

Nikki relies heavily on her family and paid help to care for the children. Although she loves them, her focus is elsewhere. Nikki says she felt she should have the ideal family and home life, so she tried very hard to create that even though it wasn't what she really wanted. This was her south node compelling her to recreate her last life's pattern.

Saturn in the 8th house indicates Nikki will not benefit from others in any way—she must look to herself to create the life she wants. In the 8th house, Saturn is clearly showing Nikki will not be looked after by others, nor can she expect them to help her financially. Saturn in the 8th house, Saturn in Cancer, and Nikki's 10th house north nodes all show that her focus should be on her career.

With her sun in the 11th house, Nikki already mixes with people she perceives to be her equals in education and lifestyle. In fact, she is involved in charitable work, and her chart suggests this is an important part of her life purpose.

Nikki's chart clearly demonstrates that enlightenment of her cosmic path early in life could have saved many heartaches and wrong turns. It also demonstrates that no matter how much we deviate from our intended path, we always return to where we are meant to be.

Saturn in the 5th House and/or Leo

Leo is the sun's natural home, so to have Saturn in this self-expressive, creative house is particularly restrictive. It not only suppresses natural exuberance, it affects self-esteem. As with all Saturn placements, there is a spiritual reason for this.

The 5th house shows how we express ourselves through artistic endeavours, our love affairs, and our children, and it shows where we derive our greatest enjoyment. It's a place of pure fun, the sort of carefree fun children have, which is why it also covers areas like days out and about, circuses, funfairs, enjoyment in its many forms, and all the ways in which we express our creative uniqueness: theatre/acting, writing, poetry, music, art, design, pottery, needlework, dress design, or any other manner of self-expression. Little is hidden in the 5th house because it wants to be admired by the world, which is why planets here are so outwardly driven to express themselves even though they are in the collective area of the chart.

Romance is a part of the 5th house, too, in the form of romantic love and casual sex. In the 5th house, we feel no barriers, and because this area is so non-judgemental and easygoing, liaisons formed are often transient. This is how we learn about relating to others; by seeing our reflection in their eyes (so to speak), we learn about ourselves too. When others love us, we see that we *are* lovable, that we have things to offer that are valuable. The more others admire us, the more we realise how special we are.

The sign of Leo is considered a self-centred one, focussed as it is on being admired for its talents—most Leos need a constant supply of praise in order to function at their best. This is often seen as a weakness, but not when we analyse the 5th house. It is perfectly natural for Leos to shine in the world; it is perfectly natural for them to need admiration that reconfirms on a daily basis that they are lovable. Leos need feedback from the world in order to comprehend their sense of self, and that is why having Saturn here is so detrimental.

Many psychologists believe problems with self-esteem stem from childhood. If you have Saturn in the 5th house and/or Leo, you probably did have issues regarding your talents and abilities from an early age. It is highly likely your self-expression was hampered as a child, and your uniqueness was not recognised by your parents. There are many reasons for this, from your parents being too busy to give you time and attention to them expecting something of you that you felt unable to fulfil. For example, perhaps you were musical but your family ran a business and expected you to take over someday, so they didn't encourage your desire to learn an instrument. In effect, your family did not recognise you as a separate, unique person with your own talents and interests—they saw you as an extension of themselves. This means you grew up not appreciating your talents because they weren't accepted by those who were supposed to love you the most. You felt your talents had no value and carried this belief into your adult life.

You have trouble in your relationships because you cannot be natural and spontaneous; you are always watching yourself and others to gauge their reactions. It's hard for those with Saturn in the 5th house and/or Leo to be frivolous—either that or you overcompensate by letting others think you take nothing seriously.

The only way you know you've done okay is when you receive outright praise. Sometimes you hold others at arm's length because you cannot accept that they truly love you. If you are spiritually unevolved, your whole life could revolve around feeling insignificant and the fear of being rejected.

Many people with Saturn in Leo have an artistic bent. Despite being proficient in one or more creative skills, it is unlikely that you will achieve worldly success. This is because of that fear of failure. You hesitate to step into the limelight out of fear of not being good enough. Alternatively, based on the other areas covered by the 5th house, it may be difficult or impossible to have children, or your personal relationships may be problematic.

Spiritual Message of Saturn
in the 5th House and/or Leo

When Saturn is in the 5th house and/or the sign of Leo, it sends a message: *You will not be required to showcase your personal talents in this lifetime because you've done that in previous lives.* The house Saturn resides is an area we are not meant to go in this lifetime, hence these restrictions. To discover your soul path in this life, check:

1. Your sun's house and sign
2. What the north nodes are saying about your life direction
3. The quadrant emphasis ("Me," "Others," collective, or individual thinking)

Saturn is placed in an area for a reason, and in the 5th house, it is highly likely that you received personal recognition for your talents and abilities in a previous life, perhaps even multiple lives. So, in this life, you are being prevented from repeating past-life experiences in order to develop other aspects of yourself more fully.

Perhaps you had a large family in the past, so it is time to think of yourself and to resist doing what comes so naturally. Relationships will also be an area of struggle, and this is because in past lives, you indulged in many liaisons. You are being asked to either concentrate on one relationship exclusively or to avoid them altogether; other placements in your birth chart will indicate which. Look to see if there are any planets in your 7th house of long-term relationships/marriage.

Once the realisation dawns that Saturn is blocking you from one area of life for a valid reason, it's far easier to adhere to your real path in life. The enlightenment this brings should lessen a great deal of the trauma of this placement.

Example: Saturn in the 5th House (In Virgo)

Steven is in his late teenage years. His Saturn is in the 5th house. He also has:

- Sun in the 10th house in Aquarius
- North nodes in the 10th house (south node in the 4th house)
- Individual thinking area emphasis

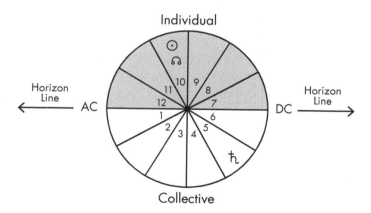

Saturn in the 5th house indicates Steven's personal talents are not important in this life—he has other things to do. Often, this means a higher calling.

Already, Saturn in the 5th is showing itself in Steven's life. He spends a lot of time alone, avoids mixing with others, hasn't yet developed any special friendships, and generally is reclusive. He doesn't express himself in any creative way, and there is a possibility he may not have, or even want, children later in life.

Although teenagers tend to be quite reclusive, Steven has always been like this: happy with his own company. However, he has a close bond with his parents, who are themselves very close, and the three of them form a unit in which he is quite happy (4th house south node comfort zone).

Saturn in Virgo indicates that Steven should not do hands-on physical work in this life. This placement is blocking him from the bottom areas of the chart, and with his sun in the 10th house and his chart emphasis in the individual thinking area, Steven's life purpose is a career. Steven is very intelligent and questioning, especially in technical matters. His sun in Aquarius means he likes up-to-date technology, and he will no doubt go on to have a successful career working with technology in some aspect.

Steven has no problem distancing himself from the self-expressive, anything-goes 5th house, because with his sun in Aquarius, moon in Libra, and Gemini rising sign—

all of which are detached, unemotional air signs—he has been given a helping hand to achieve his soul's purpose.

It seems Steven is already on the right path in life, avoiding the casual friendships formed in the 5th and concentrating on his studies. He won't seek out casual relationships either; his 7th house of marriage is devoid of planets. Therefore, whether or not Steven eventually marries, his chart shows there is no urge to form close, personal relationships.

This is quite a clear, easy chart in the sense that Steven should have no problem following the path set out for him. He is already well on his way! With the three air signs in prominent positions, Steven will always be a bit cool and detached from others. Later on, the friendships he will develop will be more selective, indicative of the planet Venus being in his 11th house. Steven may meet a life partner through selective groups, and it's likely he will go on to sit on committees and boards that make rules, regulations, and laws for others. He has a good chance of being noticed and praised for his humanitarian work.

Example: Saturn in Leo (In the 8th House)

James is in his mid-seventies and ran a successful business all of his working life. His Saturn is in Leo. He also has:

- Sun in the 10th house in Scorpio
- North nodes in the 4th house (south nodes in the 10th house)
- Individual thinking area emphasis

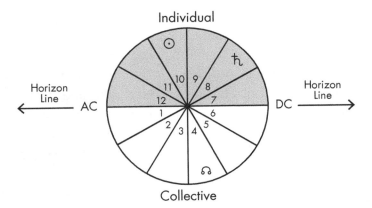

Music was a lifelong passion for James, and although he loved playing and even taught in his spare time, he had never been able to launch himself in any meaningful way using this talent. It frustrated James that even though he was confident in any and all business dealings, he had always been too nervous to play music in public, even for his own family. His Saturn in Leo indicates that this life is not one in which he can outwardly succeed with his music, because that is a form of creative self-expression.

Note that James's sun is in the 10th house, as are his south nodes, hence his natural ability to run a business. This is an interesting combination, because the south node is an area he shouldn't go back to even though it is comfortable, yet with his sun in the same house, this indicates there are life lessons about having a high-profile career that need to be learnt in this life.

With his north nodes in the 4th house, James's path was always going to diverge from the 10th house at some point—in this case, when he decided to take an early retirement. This placement indicates that James will end his life looking after others rather than being the boss, and he is already on that path, having taken up gardening and cooking as hobbies.

James's Saturn in the 8th house indicates that in this life, he couldn't rely on others to look after him. He had to make his own way in life, and that he did. James financially supported his family in numerous ways. When he retired, his task was to stop being a financial carer and become a hands-on carer, which is the message of the north nodes in the 4th house. James's wife still works, so he has changed his role and has settled into being more of a homebody.

Life manoeuvred James to where he was supposed to be in gradual steps, and the knowledge of his Saturn placement has given him an inner peace, allowing him to enjoy his music for its own sake.

Saturn in the 6th House and/or Virgo

This house is the area of hands-on physical work, the practical house of the day-to-day routines we all follow. It's called the house of service and shows, too, the psychological issues that arise when we can't find work to suit us or a place in the world where we feel our practical skills and abilities make a difference. In effect, we need to feel we matter and that we have something of value to offer.

Most of us spend our early years preparing ourselves for our working role, sometimes right up until our mid-twenties or beyond, if we follow further education to its natural end. While not all work *seems* service-orientated, it is, because we all need a roof over our head and food in our bellies—and we also work to maintain a functioning, cohesive society that we contribute to in one way or another. All work—whether for our family, home, society, or even our efforts to keep fit—falls under the sign of Virgo and the 6th house. The 6th house is the last house at the bottom of the chart, so it is below the horizon line and in the collective area.

By age point, we reach the 6th house at age thirty-five. For the next seven years, as we pass through this house, we take all our experiences and fully become an adult—we establish ourselves in a career and discover whether we are fully able to pull our own weight, both within our family and the wider family of humankind.

The 6th house, ruled by Virgo, indicates how we feel about routine. Routine is essential to most of us; it provides a framework for the day, the year, and the rest of our lives. The daily interplays between us all are found here, in regular routine.

This house also deals with mental health. Over-working, being unable to find meaningful work, being undervalued— all these situations affect mental health, and very few of us go through life without confronting them at some point. How we cope is shown in the 6th house.

Exercise and dietary regimes are also Virgo/6th house areas, as is anything that concerns the health and well-being of the physical body. If you have a personal planet here or in the sign of Virgo, you are able to focus on these aspects. Self-discipline is not a problem at all for 6th house/ Virgo people.

If you have the sun in the 6th house, you get your sense of identity from hands-on, roll-up-your-sleeves types of work. You rarely seek the limelight (the sun is in the lower half of the chart, below the horizon line), and you don't mind doing the so-called menial tasks of cleaning up, organising, timetabling, and managing finances. In fact, you may even enjoy these tasks! Anything and everything that requires attention to detail and an eye for neatness is Virgo's forte.

If you have Saturn in the 6th, this no-go area could almost be seen as a gift: Yay, no hard work! Indeed, Saturn here indicates a past life (or multiple past lives) of hard work in the service of others. But, of course, Saturn is never a picnic, and until you understand and come to terms with why Saturn is in the 6th, it can be an extremely difficult, baffling journey.

Spiritual Message of Saturn in the 6th House and/or Virgo

When Saturn is in the 6th house and/or the sign of Virgo, its message is: *You've proven yourself in this area of hard work. Now, you have another path to follow.*

The trouble is, we all need to work. It isn't simply about money, because even those who are wealthy often strive to find some sort of work, some way of feeling useful and of value. If your Saturn is in the 6th, you will feel the need for a routine more than others, yet you will also feel totally trapped by that routine. This creates frustration and, eventually, ill-health. Saturn here creates a fear of illness, which can result in extreme cases of paranoia or psychosomatic symptoms—becoming a hypochondriac, in effect.

Your work is in some way limiting for you, yet you feel that without that daily pattern, everything would fall apart and illness would rush in. It's as if you try to do what everyone else does, yet underneath you don't really relate to why you're doing it or what the purpose is. You do everything out of habit only because your heart and mind aren't in it. Sometimes Saturn's influence can be felt as a real fear of menial work and efforts to avoid it at all costs in the hopes that others will attend to it.

No matter how others try to help you overcome your dissatisfaction, they cannot because they don't understand why you feel this way, and you are unable to explain it, as it often isn't clear to you either. When others are expected to look after these aspects and you don't pull your weight, resentment is inevitable. This whole subject of work swirls with confusion and misunderstandings.

To alleviate your own suffering, you may concentrate on staying physically healthy, both in order to avoid imaginary illnesses and as a way of relieving the tension inside. However, you may take this to extremes; you're more likely to try extreme sports than to take a gentle hike.

Saturn in the 6th and/or Virgo is not meant to cause untold misery for you and your loved ones. It's here to show you that while service to others is spiritually rewarding, you've proven your expertise in this area, and there is no need to repeat a past pattern. In this incarnation, you are not meant to be in the 6th house at all, and you should avoid it. Hands-on work is not for you.

So, what is your purpose in this life? To discover your soul path, check:

1. Your sun's house and sign
2. What the north nodes are saying about your life direction
3. The quadrant emphasis ("Me," "Others," collective, or individual thinking)

It's likely that most of your planets will be at the top of the chart, showing that your path is a higher one this lifetime. The planets are also likely to be on the Me side of the chart, indicating that it is time to concentrate on yourself.

Example: Saturn in the 6th House (In Taurus)

Malcolm is in his mid-forties. He's married with one child and runs a not-very-successful car repair business. He was in prison in his younger years for being involved in someone's death; while the death was deemed accidental, Malcolm still had a long prison sentence.

Malcolm's Saturn is in the 6th. He also has:

- Sun in the 3rd house in Pisces
- North node in the 3rd house (south node in the 9th house)
- Collective area emphasis

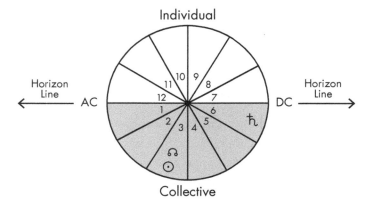

Malcolm is a special case because he spent a while in prison. Because his is a complicated chart, I've added more information in this interpretation.

Malcolm currently has a small car repair business but does not make enough to support his family; it is his wife who is the main breadwinner. The reason he struggles can be found in his birth chart—Malcolm's Saturn in the 6th house indicates he is not meant to be doing hands-on work in this life. He has more important things to do in the service of others.

Malcolm's Saturn in Taurus indicates he will have financial hardships in this life in order to learn the value of other, more important things.

Malcolm is a Pisces, and Pisces suns are generally not worldly unless other, stronger placements are in the chart. It is often hard for Pisceans to gather the emotional and physical strength for the many trials that life presents. Malcolm's moon in Aquarius is equally uncomfortable, because the mundane monotony of the essential chores of life go against his nature; Aquarians need to be different in some way.

This is obviously not an easy chart for Malcolm to grapple with. He has otherworldly personal planets, is blocked from hands-on work, and is denied financial security. So, what is his chart asking him to do? Let's look at the positives: His sun, moon, and north nodes are all in the 3rd house. The north nodes are conjunct Mercury, the planet that rules the 3rd house. Along with the collective area emphasis, Malcolm's chart points to communication as the key to his life.

His 9th house south nodes show that Malcolm is actually very wise, and this is reinforced by Saturn in the 6th. In his last life, Malcolm worked hard and learned a lot. The question is, what is it Malcolm knows so much about, and how can he use that now? Three personal planets in the 3rd house indicate to me that Malcolm could be visiting local schools and talking about his time in prison to encourage youngsters to choose a different path. North nodes in the 3rd house often signal a teacher or communicator in a community setting. Another possible career could be a counsellor to inmates or those on probation, especially as Pisces and Aquarius are both such non-judgemental and understanding signs. And, with personal experience in prison, others will listen to what Malcolm has to say. Malcolm also has Jupiter very close to his rising sign/ascendant (AC). This could be beneficial, as he is obviously not a shy person when presenting himself to people.

No matter which career Malcolm pursues, with the ruler of his sun (Neptune) placed in his 12th house, it seems likely he will have contact with the 12th house throughout his life. As this area of life has to do with isolation, either forced or voluntary, it seems far better to have contact with it via his job!

Example: Saturn in Virgo

There were two examples of Saturn in Virgo shared in previous sections. In the 4th house/Cancer section, Ben has Saturn in Virgo (page 66), and in the 5th house/Leo section, Steven has Saturn in Virgo (page 76).

Saturn in the 7th House and/or Libra

The house Libra rules, the 7th, is called the marriage house. These days it refers to any committed, long-term relationship, whether legally binding or not.

The astrological sign that begins the 7th house and any planets in the 7th will indicate the type of partner who appeals to us. It's usually very simple; if the 7th house begins in an earth sign, individuals will be attracted to earth signs. If it begins in an air sign, those are the types of part-ners individuals will seek, and so forth. But what is not taken into account is that our own rising sign—our sun sign in the last life, and how we like to present ourselves now—is 180 degrees away, and so it is effectively in oppo-sition to the 7th house.

This means we seek someone entirely different from ourselves, someone who contrasts with our personality. This may be why the 7th house is also referred to as the place of open enemies. Indeed, we probably fight more with our partner than with anyone else! This is because what draws us to someone eventually brings problems of its own. If an individual has no planets in an earth sign but their partner is an earth sign, they will never truly understand each other, even if they find their partner's differences alluring. The earth sign's desire to stay put, re-sist change, be stubborn, or focus on material things may drive their partner crazy because they cannot relate in any way. However, if the individual has a personal planet in an earth sign in their own chart, the differences won't cause as many problems because each person will be able to understand where the other is coming from.

Resolving any relationship issues that arise is the do-main of Libra. Libra is ruled by Venus, the planet of har-mony, compromise, fairness, and balance. Hence, in the

7th house, we seek to balance our own needs with those of the one we love.

The symbol for Libra shows two lines that run parallel to each other. One has a bump in the middle; relationships have many bumps to get over. The two parallel lines never actually meet—a clue that we should aim to be whole within ourselves rather than seek someone to fill in the gaps for us. However, the reality is that this is only possible for a minority of highly enlightened souls, and they generally live solitary lives without a partner anyway.

The truth is, no matter how evolved we are, we seek what we lack in others. Those who are shy and retiring generally choose a partner who is outgoing. Those who are feisty choose a quieter partner who will allow them to express their personality instead of overshadowing them. We seek in others what we cannot be, and we admire these qualities! Hence, the yin continues to seek a yang to balance it, and vice versa.

When Saturn is in this very personal house and/or sign, it causes all manner of difficulties in relationships. From the very beginning, relationships will be a challenge. Those with a 7th house Saturn and/or Saturn in Libra will still seek the qualities of the astrological sign on the descendant (DC), but their search will be overshadowed by something else: obligation and restriction. For whatever spiritual or karmic reason, they will choose someone who is bound to disappoint them later on. It's a subconscious choice. Everyone hopes for a wonderful partnership, but this is even more elusive—if not impossible—for those with Saturn in the 7th house and/or the sign of Libra. Saturn in this position inhibits the natural expression of love and the ability to compromise to bring harmony. Those with Saturn in the 7th house and/or Libra may think they are great people who are wonderfully giving and loving, but there is a coolness about Saturn that means this isn't possible.

When those with Saturn in Libra and/or the 7th house enter a partnership, they do so knowing, deep down, whether it's right or not. This Saturn position tends to make people ignore the warning bells for all manner of reasons. Eventually, these choices will result in unhappiness and isolation, for nothing is more soul-destroying and disheartening than feeling unloved, especially by the one person who is supposed to love us most. Those with Saturn in the 7th and/or Libra may blame the other person for their lack of this or that, but the truth is, they knowingly chose them. Should they walk away and then try again, chances are, if Saturn is here, the same thing would happen, but perhaps in a slightly different way.

If you have Saturn in the 7th house and/or the sign of Libra, there are various ways it can materialise. You may meet an older partner who provides stability but is controlling or manipulative with money, or perhaps a partner will mean well but cannot appreciate your point of view or values. Maybe your partner will end up being a burden, either financially or physically—something you couldn't have foreseen that was predestined to happen. Perhaps they are abusive and unkind, or unfaithful, or they gamble or drink; in some way, your partner will disappoint you. Some people make do and carry on with a sham marriage, or the partners live separate lives, only coming together when necessary. Some split and stay single, while others try again. Eventually, though, it will dawn on the Saturn in 7th/Libra person that the bonding and care that others appear to have for each other will remain elusive in any partnership they form.

If you have this placement, this section may make it sound like there is some blame attached to you for your choice of partner. That is not the case. The spiritual message of this placement is that other people are in your life for a reason, and the position of Saturn shows a karmic/cosmic lesson. There is something about this relationship (or relationships in general) that is necessary for you to learn.

According to my no-go theory, the greater cosmic lesson is that Saturn is in Libra and/or the 7th house because you are not supposed to be totally focusing on relationships in this particular lifetime. Bear in mind this does not deny you relationships, but relationships are often time-consuming and sometimes draining; those in relationships spend a lot of time placating, compromising, adapting, and loving their partner. For you, this lifetime is about something else entirely.

Spiritual Message of Saturn in the 7th House and/or Libra

When Saturn is in the 7th house and/or the sign of Libra, it sends a message: *You can have relationships, but they must not become your over-riding purpose or the be-all and end-all of your life.*

The house Saturn resides is an area we are not meant to go in this lifetime, hence these restrictions. Relationships that demand a lot of your time and effort draw you away from your real spiritual purpose, which is something other than partnership.

To discover your soul path in this life, check:

1. Your sun's house and sign
2. What the north nodes are saying about your life direction
3. The quadrant emphasis ("Me," "Others," collective, or individual thinking)

The position of your sun and north nodes will guide you to your real, proper purpose in this life, and your chart's quadrant emphasis should offer another clue.

Example: Saturn in the 7th house (In Aquarius)

Daniel is in his early twenties. He is attending university and has just split from a partner he was living with. His Saturn is in the 7th house. Daniel also has:

- Sun in the 2nd house in Virgo
- North nodes in the 1st house (south nodes in the 7th house)
- Collective area emphasis

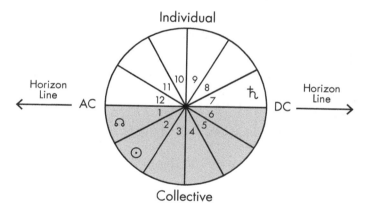

Daniel's Saturn in the 7th house indicates that a serious relationship should not be his primary focus in this lifetime.

Daniel does not find it hard to attract partners, and his easy way of connecting to others is very indicative of the south node being in the 7th house. Apparently, Daniel has had a girlfriend ever since he was about ten years old. This is because in a past life, Daniel learned how to compromise and relate to a partner (7th house south nodes); he came into this life wanting to recreate this comfortable pattern of having someone in his life.

However, Daniel's Saturn in the 7th house is making partnerships difficult in this lifetime, and it is stopping him from achieving his desired ideal relationship. He wants to settle down, but most of his girlfriends felt they were too young.

Daniel's north nodes are in the 1st house, indicating that in this life, he has to learn to stand alone in order to discover more about himself and his strengths. He is being asked to think more about himself, to develop his talents and abilities, and to look to what he wants—basically, to not see relationships as totally necessary to his well-being. Only time will tell how Daniel's relationship issues will pan out in his life, but in any case, this life is all about him, not his partnerships.

With his sun in the 2nd house, Daniel is driven to make money, so it is clear that he will have a financially successful life. He has not yet chosen his preferred career, but it looks like he will be dealing with people from all walks of life because of his sun and his quadrant emphasis being in the collective part of his chart. Presumably,

Daniel will be wealthy (the sun in the 2nd house indicates financial security, sometimes wealth), and he must resist the urge to mix only with those he perceives his financial equal. Daniel's Saturn in Aquarius indicates that he should mix with everyone.

Daniel's chart clearly shows the path he should take. While he can have partners and relationships, they should not be the be-all and end-all of his life, as they were in his previous life. In this lifetime, Daniel has to stand alone and become independent while immersing himself in the collective via his career.

Example: Saturn in Libra

There was an example of Saturn in Libra shared in a previous section. In the 3rd house/Gemini section, Sue has Saturn in Libra (page 56).

Saturn in the 8th House and/or Scorpio

Scorpio and the 8th house are difficult areas for most people to comprehend. The sign of Scorpio often confuses people, so let's have a look at that first.

Scorpio is a fixed water sign. Water signs are deeply sensitive. Fix water in one place and it forms a pool of great emotional depth—that's the sort of feeling Scorpio is dealing with. It is the most sensitive sign in a personal sense, so sensitive that any personal planet (the sun, moon, Mercury,

Venus, or Mars) in Scorpio is extremely self-protective. This is why Scorpios are so difficult to understand.

If you know a Scorpio casually, you may wonder what all the fuss is about—they seem so relaxed and fun! But if you hurt them, watch the fallout. They hide their sensitivities behind a casual, don't-care attitude when they actually *do* care, very much so. If others hurt them, Scorpios may laugh and pretend not to care, but inside they are determined to get even. They simply cannot let a hurt go, not unless they are highly evolved spiritually.

The sign of Scorpio rules the 8th house, which deals with things like death, sex, psychology, and inheritances from others. The 8th house centres around "other people" in relation to ourselves, and Scorpio rules this house because they focus their attention on getting something from others, be it money, attention, sex, worldly goods (money, houses, or *objet d'art*), or even career recognition. In order to get what they want, Scorpios have to play a part, which is a form of manipulation (Scorpio's forte). They watch the other person, decide what makes them happy (or what their Achilles' heel is), and use this information for their own ends.

Scorpios may be more than happy to give their fair share of the bargain to get what they want, so it isn't always a manipulative thing, but it is a conscious choice that involves psychology. For example, "If he wants sex with me,

I expect him to marry me" was a Victorian but widely accepted 8th house mindset. Nowadays, this type of thinking still occurs but is far more subtle, as values have changed. When two people get together to form a unit—no matter their gender, needs, or reasons—there will be an exchange of "you do this, I will do that." This is all 8th house territory.

So, if you have Saturn in the 8th house and/or Scorpio, how does this work? Put simply, you won't manage to gain anything from others in this life. No matter how astute you are, no matter how subtle (or not so subtle), no matter how hard you try to secure property or security from others, you will fail. Even if you are doing everything right, in entirely above-board ways, Saturn here indicates you will not gain inheritances, property, or large windfalls such as winning the lottery. This life is about managing on your own, finding your own way, and becoming financially responsible for yourself. This doesn't mean you cannot have relationships, it just means you won't benefit financially from them.

Spiritual Message of Saturn in the 8th House and/or Scorpio

When Saturn is in the 8th house and/or Scorpio, its message is: *You will not gain anything from others, so look only to yourself in this life.*

Saturn warns not to invest your time, and certainly not your whole life, on expectations from others. No matter how altruistic your intentions, or no matter how deeply you care or how much you do for others, you cannot rely on others for financial support. You are advised to look to build security for yourself; that is the only way it cannot be taken away from you. This is the cosmic lesson when Saturn is in the 8th house and/or Scorpio.

To discover your soul path in this life, check:

1. Your sun's house and sign
2. What the north nodes are saying about your life direction
3. The quadrant emphasis ("Me," "Others," collective, or individual thinking)

The reason you have to stand alone in this life will be somewhere in your chart. It's likely you have a destiny that you would have avoided if you were gifted wealth and property.

Example: Saturn in the 8th House (In Scorpio)

Amelia is a lady in her seventies. She was abused as a child, and she admits to marrying young in order to escape home. Amelia's Saturn is in the 8th house and in Scorpio.

(Traditionally, it is thought that Saturn in Scorpio does indicate some form of abuse. In many cases, I've found this to be sexual abuse, though not in every single case.)

Amelia also has:

- Sun in the 6th house in Virgo
- North nodes in the 2nd house (south nodes in the 8th house)
- No quadrant emphasis—planets are equally dispersed

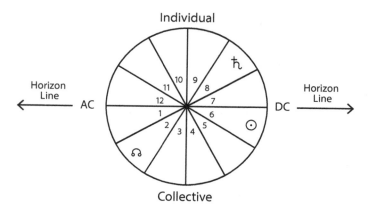

Amelia's Saturn in the 8th house indicates she won't gain from others in this life, no matter what she does. Her Saturn in Scorpio reiterates this same message.

Amelia married her first husband in order to escape a difficult home life. She says she believes she was a good wife: she stayed, had children, and played her role as expected. But when her husband died, Amelia discovered that he had left her nothing, not even the house. They had married at a time when men routinely took responsibility for the household bills and women weren't required to work. Indeed, up until the 1980s here in the UK, most women with children didn't work because there was no financial requirement. One good salary provided for the entire family, and it was considered a failure on the man's part if he couldn't fully support his wife (and a failure on the woman's part if she preferred work to being with her children). So, it was only after her husband's death that Amelia discovered he had been a secret drinker and had run up so many debts that she was left virtually penniless. She had two children to care for, no job, no income, and no roof over her head.

After a few years, Amelia married again. Although she had feelings for her new husband, she says the main reason she married him was security because life was such a struggle. When he eventually died, she found he had left his house and most of his money to his children from his first marriage. Amelia was devastated. Again, she felt she'd been a good wife, and they had a nice life, so to be left with nothing was a shock.

If we look at Amelia's chart, we see her sun is in Virgo in the 6th house of service. This is why she was such a dutiful wife and why she readily accepted the duties and responsibilities of her marriages.

Her north node is in the 2nd house, showing that in this life, she is meant to financially provide for herself instead of relying on other people. The south node in the 8th house illustrates why she expected to be helped by others: It happened in her previous lifetime. This is a very clear chart.

Amelia went on to develop a career later in life, when her children had grown up, and she did very well for herself. She finally found her way to her north nodes and stood on her own two feet in life.

Example: Saturn in Scorpio
(In the 1st House)

Sandra's life path is not dissimilar to the previous example. She is also in her seventies. Her Saturn is in Scorpio in the 1st house. She also has:

- Sun in the 6th house in Aries
- North nodes in the 3rd house (south nodes in the 9th house)
- Collective area emphasis

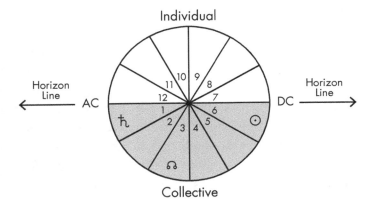

Sandra presents herself as a very reserved person despite being an Aries sun. This is hardly surprising with Scorpio as her rising sign and Saturn right on her ascendant (AC). Sandra admits to being scared of speaking in public or standing out from the crowd. Scorpio hides any weakness, so Sandra goes to a lot of effort to make sure people don't see the fears and insecurities Saturn has given her in this position. (Planets on angles—the AC, IC, DC, or MC—are particularly strong.)

Sandra's Saturn in Scorpio indicates she will never make any gains from other people and must provide her own security.

She also married young. During her divorce, Sandra found out that her husband had made unwise investments, and there was no money for her and the children when they split. She remarried a few years later after some financial hardships, and her second husband only left her a small amount of support after his death (a lump-sum pension). Although Sandra has been allowed to live out her life in her late husband's house, it is to be given to his children from a previous marriage after her death.

Sandra's Saturn in the 1st house indicates that her life is not about her, but about others. Sandra's Aries sun is in the 6th house and is guiding her to a life of service. Being such a cheerful, optimistic sun sign helped her cope with life's many disappointments, and it also gave her the energy and drive to willingly serve others in active ways.

Her north node is in the 3rd house, and coupled with her sun being below the horizon line, this indicates Sandra spent most of her life in the collective area of the chart, with ordinary people. She says she always dreamed of living in an area where she would have a more peaceful, private life (south nodes in the 9th house), but she could never financially achieve that.

Sandra's north nodes in the 3rd house indicate she has much wisdom, and she must pass it on. Indeed, later in life she was hired as a counsellor by a company that helps those who cannot afford legal fees access information and help, and she also works with another charity with similar aims.

Understanding her chart made Sandra aware that her financial difficulties weren't her fault for (in her words) "choosing the wrong men to marry," because with her Saturn in Scorpio, it was predestined that financial security from others would be denied to her.

Although we cannot know her higher purpose, she has fulfilled her destiny as foretold by her chart, and that is all any of us can do.

Saturn in the 9th House and/or Sagittarius

Gemini and Sagittarius are related signs. They are in opposition to each other across the chart, but they both deal with thought and communication. Gemini, ruled by Mercury, is the messenger of the zodiac; they flit here and there, gathering and then dispensing information. Geminis make short journeys and have no interest in delving into subjects. Sagittarius, on the other hand, rules long journeys. They enjoy going to far-flung places and do so with the aim of collecting and possibly collating information.

Sagittarians love talking to people to understand their lives in order to make sense of the world and their purpose within it. They seek the eternal truth through their own conscious thought processes and enjoy the pure joy of learning something new, as it may hold the nugget of truth that will make sense of everything. The sign of Sagittarius is ruled by Jupiter, the planet of wisdom, so they take nothing at face value. They don't necessarily believe all they are told.

Needless to say, we all have our own Sagittarian journeys of this nature, and they are intensely personal because our beliefs are personal—hence why Sagittarians are happy to do private research and live quietly in order to study. They might teach or lecture at a university, make television documentaries about their chosen subject, or become correspondents; there are numerous ways this desire for truth can be expressed in life.

While Sagittarius is a sociable sign that needs to connect with others to find out their beliefs, the inward processing of that gathered wisdom is for them alone. The 9th house is at the top of the chart in the individual thinking area, the place of conscious thought. So, while quite gregarious, they also enjoy their own company and prefer not to mix with the collective at the bottom of the chart unless it is to gather or dispense information.

Those who study astrology and similar subjects (the tarot, witchcraft, any sort of divination or mediumship, crystals, and so forth) who write esoteric books, and who give talks on obscure subjects are on the Sagittarian/9th house path in one way or another. Even religious fanatics and those who set up sects are represented here, because Sagittarius and the 9th house deal with our individual philosophy and wisdom, so this can also bring people to traditional religion. Basically, the 9th house contains the numerous paths to knowledge and wisdom, but some are blind alleys—those are for us to ascertain.

If you have Saturn in the 9th house and/or Sagittarius, it will have a profound effect on how you approach and view your own beliefs. Firstly, your beliefs will be incredibly important to you; you have a crystallised belief system that you don't want to veer from. With Saturn here, you'll be afraid of delving too deep. You are more inclined to follow an established religion because then you don't have to think about it.

Because Saturn suggests conservatism, the safe, traditional road is often taken, yet this set-in-stone belief system prevents you from moving forward in any sort of esoteric search for a greater meaning. It is likely that you solidified your belief system when you were quite young and haven't revisited it. You will find it impossible to accept those who have differing views; you may even struggle to listen to them speak. You want to persuade people that your way is the only right and true way. But faith is an individual, intuitive, private search, and being told something is right doesn't automatically make others believe the same thing; it's something they will have to decide for themselves.

Alternatively, you may believe in nothing at all. Perhaps you call yourself an agnostic. Saturn sometimes brings a sense of futility and depression; you may believe that humanity is doomed and therefore all beliefs are a waste of time.

Saturn is here for a purpose. While it often creates someone who is either an agnostic or a dogmatic believer in an established religion, this is not Saturn's purpose at all.

Spiritual Message of Saturn in the 9th House and/or Sagittarius

When Saturn is in the 9th house and/or Sagittarius, its message is: *You are not meant to be searching for your belief system in this lifetime. Other aspects in your chart will show you your spiritual direction.*

Because the 9th is an esoteric house, look for an esoteric reason why you are not supposed to access this house in this lifetime. My belief is that your past lives have given you great enlightenment, and this lifetime is about your predetermined path of practical service for mankind.

The theory in spiritual circles is that we can consciously choose to advance and heighten our angelic level by service to others. Let me explain this in more detail: Many books have been written about the realms our own spirits/souls go to after we have passed. There is a common theme amongst them that we inhabit different levels based on our actions in life. The kinder we are and the more we do for others, the higher level we achieve. Thus, serving others in any capacity is seen as a positive and helps to promote us to a higher level. These realms are described as angelic, where we leave the dense form we inhabited in life and become more light in physical and literal ways, while still maintaining our own personality and appearance (if we wish to). So, when talking of a predetermined spiritual plan, I'm referring to the spiritual time when we assess our last life and choose how to proceed in the next life in order to right any wrongs, learn new lessons, and test ourselves. This predetermined spiritual plan becomes our cosmic path, and planetary positions in a birth chart reflect our decisions. Saturn, in particular, is the planet that I believe holds the key.

To have reached the point of having Saturn in the 9th house and/or Sagittarius, you are already a very evolved soul, so it is unproductive to spend your time on this earthly plane in pursuit of spirituality.

To discover your soul path in this life, check:

1. Your sun's house and sign
2. What the north nodes are saying about your life direction
3. The quadrant emphasis ("Me," "Others," collective, or individual thinking)

Example: Saturn in the 9th house (In Virgo)

Angela is a teacher in her mid-forties. Despite her demanding career and being a single parent of two children, she has chosen to become a surrogate. One childless couple now have two children due to her kindness.

Angela's Saturn is in Virgo in the 9th house. She also has:

- Sun in the 3rd house in Aquarius
- North node in the 9th house (south node in the 3rd house)
- Collective area emphasis

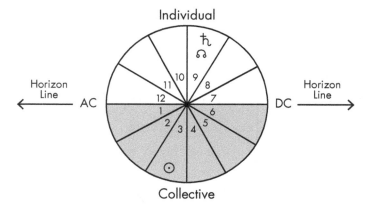

Angela is a teacher. This is a classic 3rd house sun occupation, and because both her Mars and Mercury are conjunct her sun in the 3rd house, it is not surprising she followed this path.

Her Saturn in the 9th house indicates that in previous lives, she spent time finding her own answers to life's big questions, and she is likely an old soul. In this life, it would be counterproductive to repeat this past-life pattern. This message is reinforced by her south node sign being Pisces; old souls often have a past-life link to the sign of Pisces and/or the 12th house.

Angela's Saturn is in the sign of Virgo, which indicates that she isn't here to serve others in a hands-on capacity. This makes it clear that her work must be of the mind and not the body. Although teaching small children is quite physical as well as mental, it is likely this Saturn placement is guiding her to a higher role within teaching.

This is a very interesting example because Angela's Saturn and north nodes are in the same house. Her 9th house north nodes are asking her to think about new ideas and solutions—to think outside the box—so her many years of experience will put her in a prime position to change the way people think about teaching. In some way, Angela is destined to bring new ideas into the sphere of education.

The combination of Angela's north nodes and Saturn in the same house allows her to access higher information relevant to her life path, but it stops her from living her life in the 9th. Remember that when the north nodes are in the same house as Saturn, we stay away from that house—which is Saturn's message—but we still have a task there via our north nodes.

Angela's chart is telling her that she needs to use her north node to access new wisdom, but she has to present this information via her sun in the 3rd house of teaching and education. Other personal planets in the 3rd house show this is an area of great importance in her life and draw her interest there.

It is likely that Angela is an old, highly evolved soul. She leads a very busy life serving others. At the moment, she is happy in the classroom, but in time it is likely she will be offered roles that put her in a position to do more than just teach. After all, she is destined to be an innovator in education.

Example: Saturn in Sagittarius

An example of Saturn in Sagittarius was shared in a previous section. In the 2nd house/Taurus section, Jean has a Saturn in Sagittarius (page 44).

Saturn in the 10th House and/or Capricorn

The sign of Capricorn is ambitious, focussed, and driven. Capricorns seek order, structure, and a framework in order to fulfil their potential.

Saturn rules Capricorn, but there is no denying Saturn is a hard taskmaster even when in its own sign. However, it functions better here; a planet in its correct sign works in harmony with it.

This is the only position of Saturn where we can choose—or not—to fulfil the role assigned, but if we do, it will be a hard task because we are required to do everything in a completely open and above-board fashion. If any corners are cut or if anything underhanded is done, the fall from grace will be spectacular.

If you have Saturn in the 10th house and/or the sign of Capricorn, it can go one of two ways. Either you will be driven to succeed outwardly (because Capricorn's natural home is the 10th house of career and because this sign sits on the midheaven, the highest point we can achieve in a worldly sense), or you will shun being centre-stage because of an inner fear of failure. Remember that Saturn is the fear area. Saturn in Capricorn has such a strong moral code and rigid set of personal rules that you innately fear you may not live up to your own expectations, let alone what you perceive others want from you.

If you have this Saturn placement, the reality is that you shoulder the burdens of life particularly well. Most people with Saturn in the 10th house do seek a high-profile role and lead comfortably—this doesn't mean your leadership will be beneficial for others, just that being in charge and/or being the boss is a comfortable option for you.

The desire to succeed and control is very strong with Saturn here. When harnessed negatively, 10th house energy can lead to tyranny. Spiritually, those who hold power should serve mankind and consider the best interests of all, but of course, not everyone is spiritually aware, let alone evolved.

If you are an enlightened soul, you will find it hard to really let go. You have an innate feeling you are constantly being watched by some divine spirit and judged accordingly. Thus, your life is one of work and duty. Often, what starts out as a difficult chore can in itself bring pleasure: the knowledge of having conquered yourself and the tasks you set for yourself.

Of course, not everyone abides by these personal rules. The trouble with the 10th house is its visibility in the world. Any transgression is seen by one and all. Consider modern media, in which the slightest deviation from the path is leapt on and widely advertised, and whether that deviation is deemed good or bad is often at the discretion of the media. So, while the good will be publicised, so will the bad.

The first example in this section showcases a woman whose path was decided for her by both her chart and life circumstances, but who used her Saturn in the 10th house wisely and beneficially.

Spiritual Message of Saturn
in the 10th House and/or Capricorn

When Saturn is in the 10th house and/or the sign of Capricorn, its message is: *You can choose to have a public role, but if so, you must "put away childish things."*[4]

If you have Saturn here, the real lesson is that you will lose your private identity because it's tied up in your worldly role. You are being denied the opportunity to express your true inner self by being a public figure, and while driven to be dutiful and serious in life, it is the child within that suffers. Any movement away from serious responsibility is seen as a weakness by the world at large simply because it's visible to the world at large.

When Saturn is in the 10th house and/or Capricorn, the place you are not allowed to go is back to your carefree youth. You are blocked from returning once you are established in life. You are being watched in order to become the best you can be. Those who ignore this warning do so at their own peril, because their choices will certainly be observed and commented on by the world—and this will be the thing that everyone remembers, not the myriad of good deeds you may have performed. It's likely you'll be removed from your high position, too.

For further enlightenment as to your cosmic path, check:

4. 1 Corinthians 13:11 (King James Version).

1. Your sun's house and sign
2. What the north nodes are saying about your life direction
3. The quadrant emphasis ("Me," "Others," collective, or individual thinking)

Example: Saturn in the 10th House (In Scorpio)

Queen Elizabeth II had Saturn in the 10th house. She also had:

- Sun in the 2nd house in Taurus
- North nodes in the 6th house (south nodes in the 12th house)
- Others-sided chart emphasis and collective area emphasis

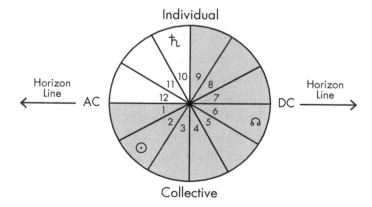

Queen Elizabeth II's Saturn in the 10th indicated she would be required to take a high-profile role in life, so she had to make sure she didn't stray from morally correct behaviour. Capricorn was her rising sign and its ruler, Saturn, was in the 10th house right on the midheaven, the highest point of the chart. It seems she was destined for greatness, even though when she was born her uncle Edward was supposed to inherit the throne of England. She had seven planets in the collective area of the chart, showing her main focus in life would be "the people."

To further cement the queen's role, she had an Efficiency Triangle (sometimes known as a T-Square) focussed on Saturn. This all-red aspect pattern showed a lot of energy and drive going into the planet at the apex—in this case, Saturn on her midheaven. Queen Elizabeth really was driven to do her job and to do it well.

With a Capricorn rising and Taurus sun (both of which are traditional earth signs), Queen Elizabeth's presentation—her hairstyle, clothes, and manner—was conservative, and her constancy was renowned throughout the world.

Her Saturn in Scorpio indicated that she wouldn't gain from others, but must look to herself in life. Of course, the queen was wealthy in her own right; she inherited her mother's estate. But when it came to the public purse, called the Sovereign Grant (the money she was paid by the British government to represent her people on the world's stage), she fared poorly. The amount was gradually reduced throughout her reign, and she was forced to give up her beloved yacht *Britannia*. This was decided by the then–Prime Minister of the UK, John Major, who announced that running the ship was too expensive. Queen Elizabeth was paying for many things out of her own pocket, but this yacht was owned by the state, so it was their decision that she had to abide by.

Queen Elizabeth's north nodes were in the 6th house of service to others, which is why she worked so incredibly hard until she was forced to step back due to ill health; by that point, she was well into her nineties. Note that her south nodes were in the 12th house, indicative of a chosen life of service. Her chart placements gifted her with a sense of duty and staying power. She really had little choice but to follow her chart's guidance.

Queen Elizabeth showed us the right way to handle Saturn in the 10th, and she stands as a shining example of pursuing her fated path with courage, strength, wisdom, and fortitude.

Example: Saturn in Capricorn (In the 2nd House)

Issy is a lady reaching retirement age who has steadily built her career to become a high-flyer in global public relations. Her Saturn is in Capricorn in the 2nd house. She also has:

- Sun in the 2nd house in Capricorn
- North nodes in the 9th house (south nodes in the 3rd house)
- Individual thinking area emphasis

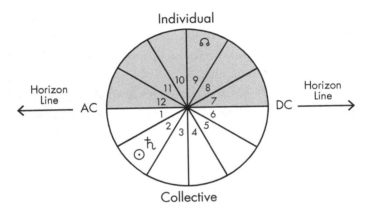

Despite Issy's years of continuous hard work and a good salary, she has failed to make the financial gains she desired, and she is disappointed she hasn't achieved more. Her Saturn in Capricorn indicated that she could have a worthy career but must do everything the correct way. However, her Saturn in the 2nd house indicates that she will not be financially successful in life regardless.

With both her sun and Saturn in the 2nd house in the sign of Capricorn—the sign Saturn rules—it was a given that Issy would work hard and strive to succeed in life. And to a certain extent, she has succeeded, reaching the pinnacle of her career and gaining a respected reputation. But circumstances have conspired against her in financial terms.

Along the way, Issy has acquired two properties, but both properties are heavily mortgaged, and she is realising that she will have to continue working long after she would have liked to retire in order to keep up on payments. The property market has slowed, and the profits she expected to make are not forthcoming.

Issy has also had three marriages, and all were failures in a financial sense. Her first husband was prone to unwise financial choices, the second was controlling with money and insisted she pay her own way, and her current husband has suffered financial setbacks since they met, so she is effectively supporting them both and paying the bills. Despite having Saturn in the sign it rules, its placement in the 2nd house of money and possessions has severely hampered Issy's ability to succeed financially.

Luckily, Issy finds great pleasure in her work, but she is disappointed she will end her life with so much less material gain than she would have liked. Yet, Issy's willingness to keep moving forward and to shoulder her responsibilities is the highest attainment of a Saturn in Capricorn. In spiritual terms, she is doing all she can.

Issy's north nodes are in 9th house, which shows that her life direction has moved from the bottom of the chart in the past life (3rd house south nodes) to the top of the chart in her current life. She is very interested in esoteric matters, and she has an open mind when it comes to spiritual ideas, which is her 9th house in action. Issy's south node in Pisces has compassion for all and indicates an old soul; she also has Mars in Cancer in the 8th, so she enjoys actively helping and supporting others. Issy volunteers to help the homeless in a hands-on role, and she is now thinking of ways that she can incorporate her business acumen, perhaps offering assistance on legal matters.

Because Issy has spent her entire life working hard, looking after her loved ones, and doing what she can to assist others, it's likely this life will be very productive in terms of spiritual advancement.

Saturn in the 11th House and/or Aquarius

The 11th house is all about friendships and groups, so one might assume it is an easier area in which to have Saturn than the more personal houses. After all, many of us don't really need the company of a lot of friends, and we may prefer not to join groups; some of us enjoy just being with our family. However, Saturn in this house does indicate difficulty in feeling at one with others, and this makes us feel isolated.

Saturn shows our fear area, so if you have Saturn here there will be a very real inability to naturally relate to other people in social or group settings, even your own family.

While you may adopt a socially graceful manner and appear to be comfortable, there will be inner feelings of separateness and isolation. You will consider yourself an outsider and act accordingly. If you didn't care about these social encounters, it wouldn't be such an issue, but you do really want to be an accepted and comfortable member of the group. Your innate shyness in these settings combined with your subconscious knowledge that you can never quite connect makes you feel lonely. After all, our world is a social one, even more so since the advent of computers, phones, and social media. Modern society assumes we are all happy to engage in these activities, and we deem it strange if a person seems to prefer their own company.

For those with Saturn in Aquarius and/or the 11th house, there is a sense of aloneness even when in a group setting—perhaps more so. There is an innate fear of not being accepted by the group and, although subtle, these vibes are picked up by others as a defensive "don't come too close" stance. So, while those with Saturn in Aquarius and/or the 11th house may be friendly on the surface, others won't seek a deeper relationship because they feel their advances are unwelcome. It is hard for anyone to really get to know an 11th house Saturn because of the vibes they unconsciously portray, which others subconsciously feel. Saturn does not function well in superficial areas, and often social groups are just that.

If you have Saturn in the 11th house and/or Aquarius, you might seem to defy this theory. If you are involved with so many groups and friendships that you hardly have time to draw a breath, this could be seen as a deliberate act to avoid deeper, more personal contacts; the activities themselves provide a conversation point, but there is no need to relate to anyone on a more personal level. Despite this, it's likely you still have a feeling of isolation and detachment. It's rare that anyone will ask to meet you privately in another capacity.

Alternatively, you may develop a superior attitude to explain your fear of belonging, with an "I'm not like everyone else" or "I'm better than everyone else" attitude, which is only a defensive stance.

Spiritual Message of Saturn in the 11th House and/or Aquarius

My belief is that Saturn is here for a reason, and that's to tell you that your life is not meant to consist of selective groups, no matter how enlightened or humanitarian those groups are. Nor should you indulge in any feeling of personal superiority as a defence mechanism. It is likely this is a past-life pattern that you repeat in every life, so Saturn is blocking it this time in order for you to find the right path and not get sidetracked by subconscious past-life memories. Saturn's message is: *Resist feelings of superiority and mix with everyone. Avoid selective friendship groups.*

Often, those with Saturn in the 11th house and/or the sign of Aquarius have a birth chart that has an emphasis down in the collective. This is to guide you to be less choosy about whom you mix with. Certainly, this life will be a learning curve regarding interacting with people from all walks of life.

It is only by analysing the rest of your chart that you can discern what your true cosmic path is. For further enlightenment, check:

1. Your sun's house and sign
2. What the north nodes are saying about your life direction
3. The quadrant emphasis ("Me," "Others," collective, or individual thinking)

Example: Saturn in the 11th House (In Leo)

John is in his mid-forties. He is a self-employed sports injuries therapist. His Saturn is in Leo in the 11th house. He also has:

- Sun in the 4th house in Capricorn
- North nodes in the 3rd house (south nodes in the 9th house)
- Collective area emphasis

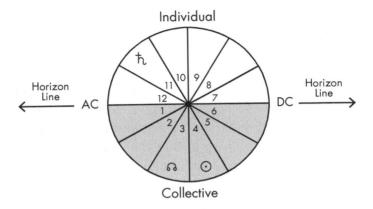

John's Capricorn sun means he strives to achieve status for himself and his family. Capricorn is an earth sign with its eye on financial rewards, advancement at work, and obtaining the material goods that hard work and persistence provide.

People with their sun in the 4th house prefer to work from home, and indeed John does. He also lives in an exclusive village even though it's beyond his financial means, and his clinic is close by, so it too has an exclusive address—a classic 4th house Capricorn sun situation.

John's Saturn in the 11th house indicates that he shouldn't be selective about who he mixes with. This is a very pertinent point, because John admits to being particular about who he spends time with. Because of this, he charges a high price for his private treatment. Despite being very gifted, his client base is modest, and he looks to his Capricorn wife to be the main earner.

John's north node is in the 3rd house, and his south node is in the 9th house. The 9th house is a comfortable place for John. He resists being down in the collective and working in a typical medical setting, preferring the isolation and independence of self-employment even though he struggles to survive financially. Living in an exclusive village and having his own private practice suits John's past-life 9th house pattern and his current sun sign and house. However, John's Saturn in the 11th exacerbates feelings of not being able to connect to ordinary people in an ordinary setting.

John's Saturn in Leo indicates this life is not about his own self-esteem. Refusing to come down into the collective and clinging to his past-life south node in the 9th house is because John likes feeling special. With his 9th house south node, there is no doubt that John is talented in his field, but his chart is saying that in this life, he should live and work in the collective area (3rd house north nodes). John should consider working at a sports or medical centre in the community; his rewards would be tangible and guaranteed, and his expertise most welcome. However, John believes his novel ideas would struggle to find a place in the more traditional methods currently used in these settings; he fears that no one would listen to him. His 3rd house north nodes are encouraging him to gradually suggest and introduce new ideas to the collective. This will lead to advances in his field, so John stands to gain a good professional reputation.

John is one example of someone following their south node pattern because it is comfortable, and ultimately, resisting their chart's path. If we all hid our light under a bushel, the world would never advance. We need people to enlighten us and advance the understanding of all, but they cannot do this if they are secluded in their ivory tower.

As difficult and painful as it may be, this is what is being asked of John. Life always manoeuvres us to where we should be, and at some stage he will be required to connect with the collective.

Example: Saturn in Aquarius

There was an example of Saturn in Aquarius shared in a previous section. In the 7th house/Libra section, Daniel has a Saturn in Aquarius (page 94).

Saturn in the 12th House and/or Pisces

The 12th house is the only house that is not seen by the world—it is kept for the individual. This is a private area, a place we go when alone. It's where we think, meditate, or contemplate beliefs and ideas.

This house is unusual in that people with their personal planets here cannot use them effectively in the outside world. While they may function in an apparently normal way, they do not gain personal fulfilment from the things that satisfy others. This especially applies to those with the sun or moon here.

By the time we reach the start of the 12th house, we are seventy-seven by spiritual age point. (See the appendix for more information on this.) It is assumed that by then, we will have done all the things required of us by our family, our peers, and the world at large. Most of us have retired from the working world. Finally, we are left to contemplate our lives in retrospect and to think about our own beliefs; we begin to make sense of the things that have happened throughout life and to analyse the bigger picture: what it was all for, the lessons we learnt, and what we now believe as we progress into older age. And, by the time we reach the 12th house, we have experienced the energies of each astrological sign and all of the planets—unless, of course, we have planets in the 12th house.

The sign and ruler of the 12th house (Pisces and Neptune, respectively) reflect this otherworldliness. The waters of life that we sprang from and eventually return to mean that the 12th house is associated with isolation and submission, and more importantly, acceptance.

The traditional view of Saturn here is that inner peace will only be found once an individual has given up their ego. Because Saturn is our fear area, this can create an irrational fear of something that cannot be defined. Usually, that fear involves losing the ability to do what we want, either through illness, mental or physical incapacity, or being imprisoned in some way, all of which leads to a dependency on others. In effect, the fear is that our choices will be taken away.

According to my new no-go theory, Saturn stops us from accessing and benefitting from the energies of whatever house it is in. It may seem strange, but it is the spiritual side of life that is being blocked if Saturn is in your 12th house. If you have Saturn in the 12th house and/or Pisces, this is an area you are not meant to go. Therefore, set aside everything you've previously read about Saturn. You are not meant to let go of your ego at all. Saturn is putting a stop sign in the 12th, probably because in past lives you already went down this spiritual path. It's very likely you are a highly evolved soul who has returned to the earthly plane to fulfil some pre-chosen cosmic path in service of mankind, or to help others fulfil their destiny in some way. You are meant to live a life of service to others, whether obvious or not.

Spiritual Message of Saturn in the 12th House and/or Pisces

When Saturn is in the 12th house and/or the sign of Pisces, its message is: *You are a highly evolved soul and you are here on earth to fulfil a chosen purpose, so don't spend time searching for meanings that you discovered in past lives. Instead, fulfil your destiny as shown by your chart.*

Often, we are in the dark when it comes to our cosmic purpose, but if you check the rest of your chart, it may become clearer. Analyse:

1. Your sun's house and sign
2. What the north nodes are saying about your life direction
3. The quadrant emphasis ("Me," "Others," collective, or individual thinking)

Example: Saturn in the 12th House (In Leo)

Anna is a lady in her early forties who currently works for a bank. Her Saturn is in Leo in the 12th house. She also has:

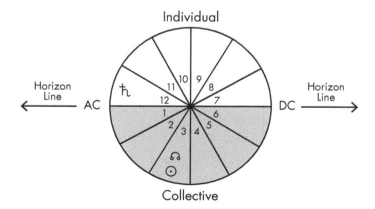

- Sun in Scorpio in the 3rd house
- North nodes in the 3rd house (south nodes in the 9th house)
- Collective area emphasis

Anna's Saturn in the 12th house indicates that this life is not about her own spiritual beliefs, but about service to others.

Anna is a hard person to get to know as her sun, Mercury, and Mars are in Scorpio, a naturally secretive sign. These planets are in the 3rd house along with her north nodes, and her quadrant emphasis is in the collective. This shows Anna's life direction very plainly; the collective area is where she gets her sense of identity (via her sun), and it is where she is meant to be.

Saturn in Leo indicates that Anna's creative abilities and sense of self are blocked. This is another clue that this lifetime is not about her.

Anna has a degree in accounting and works in a bank, but teaching is a more suitable profession according to her chart. Not only are her north nodes in the 3rd, suggesting this is her path, but a 3rd house sun is often indicative of a need to pass on information via some form of communication. Anna has taken her first step on this path by teaching English to foreign students, so it appears her life is finally headed in the right direction.

Anna's task is to avoid retreating to the 12th house and contemplating her own existence, as it seems she is already an old soul. With Saturn in the 12th house and the south nodes in the 9th, this life is about helping others by passing on her wisdom. We can't know what karmic debts Anna has or what her cosmic lessons are, but it will be through the 3rd house and communication that she will fulfil her life purpose. Often, life paths become clear with age, so while Anna is currently uncertain about her life direction, events will happen to gently guide her to where she is meant to be. All any of us can do is keep an open mind and allow the universe to take care of the rest.

Example: Saturn in Pisces (In the 9th House)

Rachael is in her late thirties. She is someone who is always willing to go the extra mile for friends and family. However, she admits that people do take advantage of her obliging nature. Her Saturn is in Pisces in the 9th house. She also has:

- Sun in Libra in the 4th house
- North nodes in the 7th house (south nodes in the 1st house)
- Others-sided chart emphasis and collective area emphasis

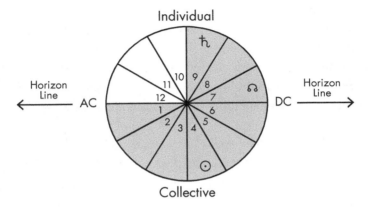

Rachael has two children by different partners, both of whom she left, and neither of whom provide any sort of support for their children. She says she prefers being alone. Her south nodes are in the 1st house, and she admits that she walks away when relationships become too demanding. Despite the difficulties of being a single parent, she finds it preferable to compromising; being independent is her south node comfort zone.

Rachael's north nodes are in the 7th house, which indicate her task in this life is to form a lasting partnership and to learn how to compromise and adapt to someone else.

Additionally, Rachael's Saturn in Pisces indicates this life is not about her personal search for spiritual meaning. Similarly, Saturn in the 9th house indicates life is not about searching for meaning. Saturn's messages in this sign (Pisces) and this house (9th) reinforce each other. Both are highly spiritual areas. Often, people with similar placements (Saturn in the 9th or 12th houses, or in Pisces or Sagittarius, or a combination) have spent previous lives in solitude or near-solitude—both houses are areas we spend time in alone.

Clearly, Rachael spent her previous life searching for answers and her spiritual purpose, and that's why she has her south nodes in the 1st house: to enable her to manage independently. This life is about more prosaic aspects: how to live her life amongst others at the bottom of the chart and how to fully connect with others, as indicated by her 4th house sun (family) and her 7th house north nodes (lasting relationships). Rachael's quadrant emphasis is in the collective/others part of her chart, so she is being asked to become an active member of her community and engage with partners.

Rachael found her chart very enlightening, and she remarked that knowing her path made her life choices much easier. She said she intends to give her personal relationships more of a chance of succeeding rather than walking away as soon as a compromise is required.

To Recap

- Saturn in the 1st house and/or Aries blocks us from showcasing our own talents, abilities, and attributes. Life is about other people.

- Saturn in the 2nd house and/or Taurus blocks us from making financial and material gains. This is to teach us that money is unimportant when it comes to finding happiness.

- Saturn in the 3rd house and/or Gemini blocks us from communicating effectively with the collective. This is because we have a higher purpose.

- Saturn in the 4th house and/or Cancer blocks us from finding fulfilment in family life. This is because we've come to rely on family and must learn to stand alone.

- Saturn in the 5th house and/or Leo blocks us from expressing personal creativity and talents. This is because this life is not about our own gifts but about what we can do for others.

- Saturn in the 6th house and/or Virgo blocks us from serving others in a hands-on capacity. We've worked hard in previous lives and have nothing more to prove in this area.

- Saturn in the 7th house and/or Libra blocks us from satisfactory long-term relationships so we have the time and space to develop other areas.

- Saturn in the 8th house and/or Scorpio blocks us from receiving money, property, and inheritances from other people. This is so we can develop our own talents and learn to stand on our own two feet.

- Saturn in the 9th house and/or Sagittarius blocks us from outwardly expressing spiritual beliefs and ideas, and it is asking us not to delve deeply into subjects. This indicates a soul that is already highly evolved.

- Saturn in the 10th house and/or Capricorn blocks us from deviating from the straight and narrow in a worldly setting. This is the highest point we can achieve in worldly endeavours, and our task is to be the best we can. Alternatively, we can choose to avoid a high-profile career and follow our sun and north node path.

- Saturn in the 11th house and/or Aquarius blocks us from selective friendships and groups. This is because this lifetime is about learning to mix with people from all walks of life.

- Saturn in the 12th house and/or Pisces blocks us from spending time searching for and expressing spiritual and religious beliefs. This indicates an old soul who has other tasks to perform in this life.

four
Saturn/North Node Conjunction

The north nodes are an accepted marker of life direction and spiritual purpose. The house and astrological sign they occupy are the guides to our cosmic path in this lifetime. Typically, people prefer the south node position (see the appendix for information on the north and south nodes) because that is the comfort area, as we lived there in previous lives. However, there is a gradual movement towards the north node house and sign as life progresses, and many people come to an acceptance of the north node area in their later years.

So, what if Saturn is conjunct the north nodes, or even in the same house? This is a valid question, because how can these two opposites be reconciled? How can you go to your north node house, yet avoid the area Saturn occupies, if they are both in the same house?

North Node and Saturn Through the Houses

My belief is that when the north node occupies the same space as Saturn, this indicates that the north node's search for meaning in that house is personal, not worldly. Read the following sections to clarify this idea.

1st House: Who We Are

This 1st house is the rising sign, and in my previous book, *Secrets of Your Rising Sign*, I put forward my theory that we relate instantly to our rising sign because it was our sun sign in the previous life. In this life, we continue to display its qualities to others while we adapt to our new chart, which gifts us with the planetary energies required to fulfil this life's task.

If your Saturn is in the 1st house, it's a clear message that this life is not one for pushing yourself into the limelight. In effect, this life is not about you at all—it's about what you can do for others.

When the north nodes are here too, this shows there are still aspects of your character that need full integration, but this will be done privately, not in the glare of the public eye. Your life path is personal; the things you must learn are for your own inner use. Therefore, you are not meant to be in the limelight in life, but to flit below the radar.

In this life, you are being asked to express the highest potential of your rising sign's energies. There are more details in *Secrets of Your Rising Sign*, which provides in-depth information about what is being asked of you and how to go about it.

2nd House: Finances and Property

The 2nd house, ruled by Taurus, shows how we feel about money and the ownership of property, and how we go about obtaining both. This is obviously an important house for everyone, as we all want financial security.

This is a tough place to have Saturn; it means that any money you earn will be spent on your own personal needs and will only be enough to survive on. Saturn here generally means hardship in financial terms, no matter how hard you work. This is to teach you money is not the be-all and end-all. Although humanity has put money on a pedestal and values riches, money is valueless in spiritual realms—it's who you are and what you do (and have done) that is relevant to your inner growth and advancement. Often, Saturn here shows a life path of spiritual enlightenment.

When the north nodes are also in the 2nd house, they indicate you have lessons to learn about how to rely on yourself for money and not to expect it from others. This placement also teaches you to value yourself for what you can give to others: What can you do for others that does not involve finances? Real riches come from who you are, what you do, those who surround you, and the love and support you all offer each other. Having the north nodes and Saturn in the 2nd house shows this is your area of greatest hardship, but it also offers the greatest personal rewards. Try to embrace the lessons and learn from them.

3rd House: Communication

This house is all about communication on a daily basis. It deals with friends, siblings, early education, and all interactions that form links between people: having a coffee in a café with a friend, sharing gossip or advice, and nowadays it also covers all forms of social media.

Saturn here will block easy communication of this sort, so its likely you feel happier discussing technical or scientific subjects than personal matters. It also blocks you from accessing social media, so any attempts to make a name for yourself or promote a business in this way will not be very successful or profitable. This Saturn position is telling you not to engage in social media and mindless gossip or chatter; your path is one of higher learning.

If you have the north node in this same house, it will be teaching you how to communicate effectively all the while. There will be some area that needs work; maybe you need to lecture on a subject or write articles? Basically, you have to find a way of connecting with others through the 3rd house while making sure you are using your talents in a higher way. When this area is blocked by Saturn, it is often through the 9th house that communication is allowed, but this means you need to be an expert on a subject before attempting to access the 9th house to share your wisdom with others.

These two conflicting aspects are both funnelling you into the correct way of using language to fulfil your life tasks. To find out what these life tasks are, check your sun's sign and house, the quadrant emphasis, and where Mercury (the planet of communication) is.

4th House: Home and Roots

When Saturn is in the 4th house, it suggests there were some issues with your upbringing that made it a cold and lonely place; you may have felt unloved. Alternatively, you could have had a lot of love, but a parent (or both of your parents) was busy, working away, or otherwise occupied, so they didn't give you enough of their time. Because the 4th is a very subjective house, it may be that you were loved very much, but you perceived a coldness or disinterest, or maybe you are not a demonstrative person anyway. (Maybe you have a lot of planets in air signs or otherworldly placements in Aquarius or Pisces.)

The north node here means this lifetime is about coming to terms with your upbringing. It's guiding you to acceptance and forgiveness of your childhood trauma, bringing an awareness that nothing in life is perfect—even your parents, who are, after all, only human and have all the same failings and frailties as everyone else.

Even so, your happiness is not to be found in the home and family in this life because Saturn is placed here. Instead, happiness will be found through other aspects/areas of your chart. Look at what the rest of the chart is saying: Your sun sign and house, the quadrant emphasis, and maybe the moon too (because it rules this house) are a guide for where to direct your energies.

5th House: Creativity and Self-Expression

The 5th house deals with ways of being creative, from acting, painting, writing, sculpting, playing an instrument or composing music, dressmaking, and all the associated areas of creativity, to giving birth (an act of creation) and the general enjoyment of life. When Saturn is here, it will block your free expression in some way. It also stops your natural exuberance and the ability to let go and just have fun.

This house is about self-esteem. Whatever talents you have will not be recognised by the world with Saturn here, so no matter how gifted you are, you will never manage to achieve recognition of your abilities. When Saturn is in the 5th house, this lifetime is not about showing your talents to the world, and when the north node shares this house, there will be a lot you have to learn about expressing yourself in creative ways. Saturn always blocks outward movement. You are being advised to find a way to experience personal pleasure in your own creative endeavours while accepting that this life is not about showing others what you can do.

There will be a reason for this. Check the sun's position by sign and house, the quadrant emphasis, and the house and sign of Mars, which will guide you in the direction your outward energies should be used to fulfil this life's purpose.

6th House: Work and Service

This house is about the hands-on, manual work done on a daily basis. Generally, it's unsung work, like household tasks: any unpaid and unremarked physical work that helps others but is usually taken for granted and rarely appreciated. This work is done because it's required, and the reward is the personal satisfaction of a job well done.

The 6th house also covers bodily health, both physical and mental.

If you have Saturn here, it can make you a hard task-master (both of yourself and of others) because you equate order and routine with safety. You often tolerate jobs and situations even when you aren't happy in them because you'd rather do that than challenge the status quo. Sometimes this can result in ill health—physical or mental—or you can end up resenting the amount of work you do; in effect, you can become your own worst enemy.

When the north nodes are also in the 6th house, they indicate that this life is about learning how to serve others without the expectation of reward or praise. Both Saturn and the nodes in the 6th show that your life is about finding ways to serve others that make you feel both useful and of value—not ways that make you feel like a doormat or undervalued.

The best way of combining the two is to look outward and help those in the community, maybe by doing volunteer work or something for charity. Use your helping skills in ways other than actual menial work; this way, you are fulfilling your north node path while avoiding Saturn's pitfall of making yourself ill serving others.

All things are noted in the spirit world, so no kind act goes unrewarded or unnoticed there. This work will make you feel a valued member of the community who has something to offer. Check the sun's position by astrological sign and house, the quadrant emphasis, and look to Mercury, the ruler of this house, as a guide for where to invest your energy.

7th House: Long-Term Relationships

Saturn in the 7th house shows that long-term relationships and the more formal commitment of marriage are areas of the greatest challenge for you in this lifetime.

Most people with this placement have difficulties with relationships. This could be due to your reasons for choosing a partner in the first place (usually there are practical reasons as well as love/friendship), or partners may become a burden in some way; maybe you chose someone older or your partner becomes ill and needs care. This is not to say you won't have relationships, but what starts out promising tends to deteriorate in one way or another.

Whatever the reason, or however it happens, Saturn is saying this life is not about your partnerships, but about some other aspect of your life. Relationships are time-consuming; there is a lot of give-and-take and compromise required, and this may draw you away from your cosmic life task.

However, when the north nodes are also in the 7th house, you still have lessons to learn about relating to others. It might be advisable to share your life in some way, either through a business partnership or a close friendship, without involving yourself in a total commitment. In this way, you will learn how to compromise and share without a time-consuming, lifetime partnership.

If Saturn and the north nodes are both in your 7th house, it's likely a lot of planets will be on the Me side of the chart or at the top, showing your life is meant to be a personal journey of some sort. Check the sun's position by sign and house, the quadrant emphasis, and even Venus, the ruler of this house. All of these aspects will show you where to direct your energy.

8th House: Sex, Death, Inheritances, Psychology, and Other People's Belongings and Values

The 8th house covers a lot of areas, but the bottom line is that it deals with what other people have, up to and including their values and beliefs. Other people's values are important because if you are financially supported by someone or work for them, you have to accept their beliefs and values, at least outwardly.

This house is about what you can get from others, which always involves either a spoken or unspoken exchange: "I will do this, and in return, you will do that." Sex is 8th house territory because, particularly in the past, women provided sex in return for marriage and security, and men provided financial security in return for sex.

When the north node is also in the 8th house, its lessons have to do with who you choose to give yourself to and why, as well as the aforementioned areas of death, inheritance, and values. There are lessons to be learnt and a path to follow that involves one of these areas. Perhaps you have lost all your money and must gratefully accept help from others, and in return, you will have to play a role expected by your benefactor.

In some way, the exchange between you and another will be a learning curve in this life. Despite being independent, you will be required to abide by someone else's rules.

Saturn in the 8th house blocks any gains from others, especially financially. No matter how much you do for someone, you will get nothing back—or maybe you will get very little, certainly less than was expected. You may spend a lifetime serving someone else only to find the expected rewards do not come. Still, the lessons have to be learnt with the north nodes here.

Check the sun's position by astrological sign and house, and locate Pluto, the ruler of this house, as both planets will indicate where to direct your energy. Also look at the quadrant emphasis for more information.

9th House: Personal Philosophy and Wisdom

This house is all about learning taken to a higher level, a higher consciousness. It's about the search for the truth and finding your own meaning of life. This can involve long, physical journeys (short journeys are covered by the 3rd house) to discover other cultures or to uncover mysteries in archaeology or ancient history; it can mean studying esoteric subjects; it can even indicate quiet, private study. Religion, philosophy, and linguistics are all topics that you can use to find your own answers to the meaning of life.

Saturn in the 9th house blocks the desire to search for a deeper meaning, often because of a fear of finding out something you don't want to know. The usual result is believing in nothing at all, or clinging fervently to a traditional religion that offers all the answers so that you don't have to think for yourself.

The fear of Saturn can run so deep that even the idea of travelling to a foreign location can be scary. Or maybe you do travel but only to enjoy the sun rather than to explore how other cultures live and think. In every way, Saturn stops your search for meaning and truth. Yet, when the north node is also in the 9th house, it is saying this is the place you must learn about, so how can you do both?

Check out the sun's position by sign and house, the quadrant emphasis, and the position of Jupiter, the ruler of this house, as guides for your life's direction. Very often, those with Saturn and the north node in the 9th house have their sun at the bottom of the chart, in the collective area.

The nodes are pointing to thinking outside the box in order to bring new enlightenment to a subject of interest—usually something that can help you in your career and advance human thought in a particular area—rather than spending your whole life searching for your *own* meaning. With Saturn and the north node here, it's quite likely you are already an enlightened soul.

10th House: Career

The 10th house is the pinnacle of worldly success that you can achieve. Along with recognition and praise comes status and the concomitant rewards.

When Saturn is in the 10th house, it creates a fear of failure. Because failures in this house are visible to the world, there is no sneaking away from exposure and shame. So, you either avoid a high-profile role or launch into it with the aim of making a name for yourself. But be very careful to do everything properly and above-board, with no corner-cutting; do everything with the good of other people in mind, or you will fail.

Those of you who also have the north nodes here should follow the higher path of the 10th house because that is your role in this life. This difference (being allowed to experience this house rather than avoiding it) is because Saturn rules Capricorn and the 10th house, so it's in its happy place. So, you should focus on this house, but only with the very best intentions and for the good of all. The north nodes here are a reminder to be the best you can be because whatever you do is visible and on display for everyone else—there will be no hiding place and no shirking of moral responsibility.

11th House: Chosen Friendships, Groups

The 11th house is on the left-hand side of the chart, so it is about personal choice. This area concerns the selective groups and societies that we can join to be with others of like mind. There is less of a desire to relate to others in a one-on-one relationship and more of a desire to be part of a group with shared ideals and interests, some of which aim to do good for society. This is the humanitarian house ruled by Aquarius.

When Saturn is here, it suppresses the desire to be with groups and creates a feeling of separateness and, sometimes, isolation from others, either because you feel unwelcome or are too shy to participate. The reason Saturn does this is to show you that this is not your path in this life. Often, those with Saturn in the 11th house have an emphasis at the bottom of the chart, so the desire to keep yourself removed from life is not going to happen. Instead, you will be encouraged to mix with everyone, not only those rarefied groups.

However, when the north nodes are also in the 11th, there are still lessons for you to learn about the 11th house and group friendships. Maybe you can take the ideas and ideals from the group (the upper part of the chart) and present them to the collective (the lower half of the chart)?

Check the positions of the sun by sign and house and the quadrant emphasis for more clues as to your life direction. Also check where Uranus is, because that planet rules the 11th house.

12th House: Spiritual Beliefs

This house is the furthest away from the outside world and is for our own private access. It is the 12th house where we form our own beliefs while alone in quiet contemplation. Any institution that is removed from the busy commercial world—such as prisons, hospitals, and religious retreats—are found in this house. This is because in these places, contact with the outside world stops, so one has the time and space to think.

Not everyone is required to partake in life, and some choose not to. Some people voluntarily choose to escape via drugs or drink. People who live on the fringes of society are actually living in the 12th house. Sometimes we take a step back from society during retirement, when we find ourselves more isolated from the stream of life. Separation also comes with age, as we generally end up on the sidelines.

My belief is that when Saturn is in the 12th house, it is because you have already achieved spiritual enlightenment. You have returned to this life in order to serve mankind. Therefore, it's counterproductive to spend time in this area, hence the no-go sign.

When the north nodes are also here, though, this means there is still something important about the 12th house that you need to discover or do. Sometimes it means giving up your own personality in order to serve a higher cause. This house is about finding your beliefs, and if the nodes and Saturn are here, they indicate a life of service. Follow your heart and mind and do what feels right for you.

If you have any doubts, look at the sign and house of your sun as well as your quadrant emphasis. The position of Neptune will also be a clue, as it rules the 12th house. The house Neptune is in indicates the area of life where you should be focussing your 12th house energies.

five
Saturn Conjunct
the Planets

When you generate a birth chart online, the website will identify conjunctions. The website I use shows an orange block linking two planets when they are conjunct. Conjunctions are when planets are so close to each other that their energies combine.

While conjunctions typically occur if planets are up to 10 degrees away from each other, Saturn has a 5 degree orb. This means that Saturn will not impact any other planets until they are within 5 degrees of each other, and the closer they are, the stronger the impact.

Saturn will affect us more deeply when conjunct the personal planets (sun, moon, Mercury, Venus, and Mars), with the sun and moon being particularly affected. It affects us a little less so when conjunct the outer planets. Each position has its own particular message regarding one's life path.

In this chapter, I've given chart examples for Saturn conjunctions that have a powerful impact, like the sun and moon. These are often more complicated to interpret, so real chart examples do help us understand these conjunctions.

Sun/Saturn Conjunction

When considering my new no-go theory of avoiding the area Saturn is in, a sun and Saturn conjunction can cause great confusion: If the sun is how we express who we are and Saturn says we shouldn't, how are we to interpret this?

The sun is the most important planet in the birth chart. The astrological sign it is in shows our primary energies and our drive in life, and the house it is in shows the area of life where we will be most motivated to use our sun sign.

Saturn conjunct another planet has a strong influence on that planet. It suppresses it. How can the sun shine if Saturn is always watching over its shoulder, warning it of caution?

It will come as no surprise to learn that people with these two planets conjunct often have trouble expressing their full personality. If you have a sun/Saturn conjunction, your whole life will feel like a struggle, as if everything has to be earned the hard way, be it money or relationships. You learned early on that nothing comes easy or without a price. There is an innate sense that anything worthwhile demands a sacrifice, which is why those with this conjunction tolerate far more in the workplace, in relationships, and from other people than the rest of us. Saturn both creates these difficulties in your life and gives you the staying power to deal with them. In some ways, you make a rod for your own back because Saturn gives you the inner fortitude to stay in situations others couldn't tolerate.

Saturn's Capricorn shading instils the sun with a serious, worthy, and earthy appearance and attitude, regardless of the sun's astrological sign. Saturn's influence seems to dull even the brightest, most vibrant sun to the extent that it cannot shine in the way it should. When the sun and Saturn are conjunct, people carry a heavy sense of responsibility.

Because those with a sun/Saturn conjunction have a reassuring presence, you unconsciously lure those who take advantage of you: *I can't manage life, but look! Here is someone who can carry the burdens for me!* Thus, you end up with even more responsibilities and burdens. Fragile people are drawn to you like iron filings to a magnet. But the weak are so draining they can destroy a sun/Saturn person, or at least take them to the brink.

There is always a reason for Saturn's position in a birth chart, especially when conjunct an important planet like the sun. This is not random. Before beginning this life, you chose a life path that made this planetary conjunction necessary. I believe the reason for this conjunction is that in past lives, you sidestepped or abandoned your previously agreed upon obligations. This is not in any way a judgemental comment—it's okay to decide enough is enough and leave a truly difficult situation! You may have set yourself too hard a task in a previous life, one impossible to achieve. The spirit realm is always compassionate, and at some stage, you chose to have another go at life to get it right. To keep you true to your course this time, Saturn was placed conjunct your sun.

Saturn conjunct the sun is a sure sign that this life is a particularly karmic one. This conjunction was a consciously chosen agreement prior to this lifetime. It may seem like a strange idea, but Saturn is there to help, not to hinder. Saturn steers the sun to be grounded, realistic, and stable, regardless of the sign it's in. It ensures tremendous staying power. Think of Saturn conjunct the sun as a helping hand to undergo and survive the trials that life is asking you to confront.

No one can fully understand the subtle ways this will manifest in life or the exact lesson being explored, but Saturn is conjunct the sun to encourage you to stay on your pre-chosen path. It is giving both the necessary restriction and also the strength to face your life lessons.

The following example demonstrates one way the sun/Saturn conjunction can present.

Example: Sun/Saturn Conjunction

Alan has just turned forty. He is a gifted design engineer. He has:

- Sun/Saturn conjunction in the 4th house
- Mars in the 2nd house
- North nodes in the 10th house (south nodes in the 4th house)
- Collective area emphasis

The first thing to note is that not only are Alan's sun and Saturn conjunct in the 4th house, but his south nodes are there too, so it is clear this is the area of his life lessons. Let's try to unravel all these layers.

The sun in the 4th house indicates this is the area of focus in this lifetime. Alan's most important life lessons will be confronted and dealt with in the 4th.

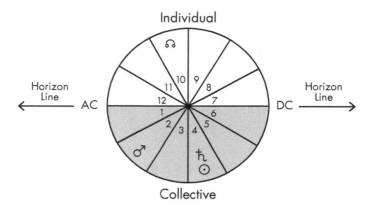

Saturn's presence in the 4th house indicates that in previous lives, Alan failed to extricate himself from the family ties that bound him so tightly. This time, to ensure the correct path is followed, Saturn is hampering his sun—his sense of self—from fully integrating into the family.

When Saturn is in the 4th house, individuals often felt isolated as children, no matter how deeply they were loved. Circumstances occurred that somehow separated the parents from the child, if not emotionally, then physically. This feeling of a lack of love and care was carried into adulthood. As we consciously and unconsciously use our own upbringing and parents as role models, it will be extremely hard—if not impossible—for someone with Saturn in the 4th to create their ideal family.

When he was young, Alan's family moved abroad, but his mother and father separated shortly afterwards. Alan had the choice of whether to live with his father or mother. Because he liked his new school abroad and had made many friends, he decided to live with his father during term time and return home to his mother during the school holidays.

Alan had parents who cared about him very much, but his father spent a lot of time working away from home. When Alan's father was at home, he was fairly detached. (He was an Aquarius sun.) Alan's mother, being in a different country, was not there to support him when he required it. Thus, Alan felt abandoned, displaced, and sometimes neglected even though he was loved by both of his parents. This is a really good example of Saturn in the 4th.

With Alan's seemingly complicated selection of planets and positions, he is being guided to detach himself from close ties to his family. This will seem strange because the sun is also in the 4th house, but it is indicating that this is the area of Alan's most extreme challenge in life: his desire for a family, yet his inability to form one that will bring him true contentment. He is being forced to analyse, time and again, his dependence on his family.

When Alan was in his twenties, he had a disastrous relationship. It lasted a long time due to his inability to walk away. The woman was controlling and manipulative, and she forced him to cut ties with his friends and family. She appeared a strong person but was looking for someone to protect her from life; she had emotional issues, which meant she had trouble relating to others. She saw Alan as her rock, as someone who could protect her from having to deal with people, and he felt too guilty to leave her. This is a common theme with a sun/Saturn conjunction in the 4th: A weaker person is drawn to the strength of the sun/Saturn person who doesn't want to inflict pain or hurt, so they tolerate a difficult and restrictive relationship.

Already, we have two situations where Alan's home life was disrupted: as a child and as a young man. In this life, Alan is literally being denied a happy home. No home and family he forms will ever feel quite right, and while he may continue in a partnership or have children, there will always be a sense of duty and responsibility—sometimes unwelcome—that this conjunction will evoke. Saturn gives a sense of coldness and inability to relate, so while Alan's family were obviously supportive and loving in the normal sense, it is Alan's Saturn that inhibits his ability to accept what they provided as proof of their love.

Eventually, it will dawn on Alan that investing his time, energy, and resources on a family is not his path. His contentment and happiness in life will come from relying on himself alone. His path is clearly marked via his 10th house north nodes, and he has an efficiency triangle focussed on his Mars in the 2nd house (the area of money and property). By finding a career that utilises his considerable talents and strong work ethic, Alan will find both financial stability and contentment.

Because Alan has a collective quadrant emphasis, he will find this lucrative career while working with others in the community. He could also work from home more, which would feel comfortable with his sun in the 4th.

Alan can certainly have relationships, but he needs to view them as secondary to his life path. He should avoid getting swept up in the emotional dramas of family life. Hopefully, he will break the chains of past-life karma that makes this 4th house such an area of focus and challenge for him in this lifetime.

Moon/Saturn Conjunction

The moon is a very sensitive planet. It shows how we feel and where we get our nurturing from. Every time we see, feel, hear, or experience something that is pleasing, it is in some manner the moon's domain. For example, a moon in Taurus person might find peace and pleasure when in the countryside, when warm and cosy, and when secure and safe, though they might not realise it is the moon being activated that makes them feel that way.

The moon is the child within all of us, so it is a very tender area. Put stern Saturn beside the moon and it creates a block to more sensitive feelings, quite apart from the struggle to find pleasure in all the things that should comfort us.

Those with a moon/Saturn conjunction certainly have feelings, but it will be hard to outwardly express those feelings and emotions. If you have this conjunction, you fear that you will be mocked, ridiculed, or dismissed, so you tend to deny your feelings, clamp them down, and refuse to admit you are sensitive to anything at all. Psychologists claim a difficult childhood is to blame for being unable to express this part of ourselves, but the moon/Saturn conjunction was in your chart from the moment of birth. It is an innate predilection, so this fear cannot only be because of the way you were treated as a child. However, if we assume pre-life choices were made, this was a deliberately selected position of Saturn; thus, your family was also chosen for just this reason. Your family's suppression of emotions and their expectations that duty, responsibility, and structure would take the place of emotion were all part of a pre-decided and agreed-upon plan. This plan allowed you and your family to learn certain lessons and to grow in knowledge, wisdom, and enlightenment.

The moon/Saturn conjunction indicates that you were supposed to have difficulties as a child, and they were for a reason. It is normal not to know the true whys and wherefores of this position. It requires a measure of faith and trust that the things that happened to you, good or ill, are relevant to your spiritual growth, and they served a purpose.

Many books have been written about how to overcome the restraints Saturn places on the moon and emotion. Psychologists and counsellors have suggested ways to overcome emotional blocks and to learn to allow the flow of emotions and feelings full force. But this is unlikely to happen. Throughout your life, you will live with Saturn suppressing your moon—you won't suddenly find you have no problem expressing your emotions. Even after years of analysis and confrontation, you will never get rid of Saturn. Psychology and/or counselling may provide coping mechanisms, but it won't remove Saturn from your chart.

My belief that Saturn indicates where not to go provides a better solution because of the fact you cannot ever just "get over" your difficulties expressing emotion. Once you accept that Saturn is conjunct the moon for a reason, there will be a new enlightenment. Your feeling nature is not the issue in this lifetime; there is another solution to your problems that doesn't involve your emotions.

So, assuming this conjunction has been pre-decided, why? We cannot know for sure, but I would guess that you were overly emotional in previous lives, or your emotions were so strong that they hampered you from fulfilling your pre-agreed course of action in life. In this lifetime, you are very clearly being shown that your emotions have to be restrained and that giving them free rein is counter-productive to your life path. To understand why is only possible if you analyse the rest of your chart. Where is the sun, where are the north nodes, and what is the quadrant emphasis?

When Saturn is conjunct the moon, the containment and withholding of excessive emotions and feelings are the key to your life path. In today's world, this might seem strange, but throughout the ages humanity has both encouraged and denied the expression of emotions, with the outward expression of feelings being more acceptable at certain times than others. Each country also has different beliefs regarding showing emotions. In the past few centuries, showing feelings was discouraged, certainly here in the UK. People were not supposed to give in to fear and worry or dwell too much on themselves. The phrase "a stiff upper lip" was consciously followed by all classes of society. Boys and men, in particular, were not supposed to cry or give in to their fears; it was considered weak for anyone to show excessive emotion, but especially men.

Today, people are allowed—indeed, encouraged—to express their needs, desires, and wants and to actively pursue their own happiness. Hence, people with Saturn conjunct the moon are misunderstood. Very often, they are encouraged to be more open and outwardly affectionate. This will not be possible for someone with this configuration, and asking them to be someone they're not could be harmful for their spiritual development.

Spiritual teachings have always encouraged people to be more compassionate, understanding, and non-judgemental, but they have also advised a detachment from emotions. Many famed Eastern mystics lived alone or meditated alone, and the suppression of personal emotions was a necessary factor in obtaining enlightenment. Detachment from human emotions is a highly valued spiritual achievement. Instead of feeling sorry for those with a moon/Saturn conjunction or trying to force them to express their feelings, we should be envying them, because they've been given the key to real spiritual enlightenment.

Example: Moon/Saturn Conjunction

Alexis is in her late twenties. She has:

- Moon/Saturn conjunction in the 8th house
- Sun in the 2nd house in Taurus

- North nodes in the 10th house (south nodes in the 4th house)

- No quadrant emphasis

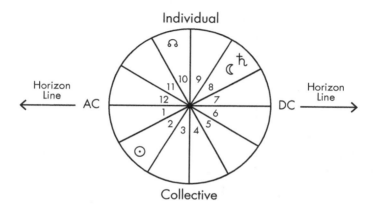

Alexis has her moon/Saturn conjunction in a very sensitive house. The 8th house is really about what we get from others, and Saturn here blocks her from receiving any material wealth from others no matter how hard she serves them or how hard she works.

Because Alexis's moon is in the 8th house, this will create real emotional difficulties for her. It would appear that in her previous life (or lives), she relied heavily on others to support her, so she still has an emotional attachment to being cared for by others.

Her sun is in the 2nd house in Taurus, and Alexis admits to being very materially minded. She is driven to be financially secure, yet she feels she doesn't have the personal tools to be able to do this for herself. Alexis left school as soon as she could and worked in fashion retail, so she feels her earning ability is not commensurate with her security requirements. What she would really like, she admits, is a husband who will support her.

In today's world it is not a given that a woman will be fully supported by a partner, as most people are expected (and usually required) to work. Alexis said the sort of man she would like—one who could provide the material security she ideally prefers—wouldn't look twice at a normal girl like her (in her words). She added that in today's climate, it felt wrong to express her desires in this area. This is Saturn in the 8th house in action: Alexis's fear that she won't be able to access this house and support from others, despite having an emotional need (with her moon here) to be cared for, and her fear of expressing these needs to a possible partner.

With Alexis's north nodes in the 10th house, it is clear that a career is her life path, and her south nodes in the 4th house of home and family indicate her comfort area, which is why she wants to repeat this past-life pattern. Her south nodes are also in Cancer, which makes her a natural carer of others. However, her north nodes in Capricorn show Alexis's career successes will come later in life. As time goes on, she will move from her caring Cancer south node towards her more professionally driven Capricorn north node. Interestingly, Alexis shares that she does enjoy her job but isn't motivated to strive for a management position.

Alexis's moon is in Scorpio. When situated in the 8th house, those with a Scorpio moon often use subtle—and not so subtle—ways of getting their needs met using manipulation. This could be as simple as crying when they don't get what they want to extreme forms of control and emotional blackmail. Alexis and I discuss the possibility that in previous lives she may have used her moon to get her needs met. She admits she was adept at getting what she wanted in most situations. We then talk about why, in this life, this won't work for her: Alexis is being blocked from using her moon's energies in this way, and she is being shown that her life path involves finding her own abilities and learning to work hard in a career.

Although Alexis is disappointed her life is heading in a different direction than she would prefer, our conversation opened her eyes to her real purpose and path. We discuss what she enjoys doing and whether she can find a different job that she would feel more motivated to achieve success in, and I remind her that a husband and family are available to her should she so choose, but that she must still strive for a career and her own financial security.

Mercury/Saturn Conjunction

Mercury is the planet of thought and communication. How we think and the way we speak is defined by the astrological sign Mercury is in when we are born, and the house Mercury is in is the area we use as a conduit to the outside world when expressing our thoughts and words.

When Mercury is in a fire sign (Aries, Leo, or Sagittarius), individuals express themselves forcefully and intuitively. Just think how a fire, once lit, rapidly burns and spreads. These signs tend to speak fast and rarely consider what they are about to say; the focus, too, is often on themselves.

The earth Mercury signs of Taurus, Virgo, and Capricorn are slower in their reasoning processes simply because they think things through, which fire signs rarely bother to do. If a fire sign Mercury gets something wrong, they can handle it. But earth signs take their time because they don't want to make a mistake, as mistakes waste time, energy, and resources.

Those with an air sign Mercury (Gemini, Libra, or Aquarius) have logical minds, with the communication of ideas and thoughts their main aim. They actively avoid emotionalism in discussions.

When Mercury is in a water sign (Cancer, Scorpio, or Pisces), individuals communicate via emotion and compassion towards others. They tend to use their feelings when thinking and expressing their ideas.

Any planet that comes into contact with Saturn is considered repressed, so it is easy to see that Mercury, the planet that rules how we think and communicate, will be strongly affected by a conjunction with Saturn.

Let's first consider benefits this conjunction may have. Regardless of the astrological sign the planets inhabit, a conjunction between Mercury and Saturn will provide the benefits of common sense, reason, logic, thoroughness, caution, and wisdom in both business and financial matters. If you think of this conjunction as a Capricorn Mercury, you won't be too far off the mark in your interpretations.

As being astute and wise in business is not a drawback in our world, you may not find many people complaining about having Mercury conjunct Saturn. However, the rest of the chart needs to be analysed to see whether sensible, rather dour Saturn helps or hinders the individual.

Fire Sign Mercury/Saturn Conjunctions

Having a little dose of Saturn when you have an Aries Mercury might not be a bad thing. Aries are renowned for being straight-to-the-point chatterboxes. Being the first sign of the zodiac, Aries generally talk about themselves. If you have an Aries Mercury, you are brimming with new ideas and plans, and you don't like to be thwarted or told an idea might not work. You aren't interested in the negatives because if things do fail—though you don't think for one minute that they will—you can handle it. And anyway, there's always another idea on the back burner.

If Saturn is conjunct your Aries Mercury, this will have a huge impact on your joyful optimism, making you more cautious, more careful of your expressions, and more sensible when planning new ideas. In some ways, it is a pity to see such bright optimism dulled. On the other hand, Saturn, as the wise parent advising caution, could make for a really good business head, and along with the Aries drive to start projects, this could be a good balance of energies.

Those with a Leo Mercury shine like the sun itself, which is apt, as Leo is ruled by the sun. Leos are meant to be centre stage, in the spotlight, being admired by one and all. There is no doubting their charisma and charm. Add Saturn into the mix and you have a different person altogether. Traditional astrology assigns this as the most difficult position for Saturn to be because of the fragile nature of Leo's ego. (Refer back to the section on Saturn in the 5th house and/or Leo to refresh your memory about how Saturn affects Leo.) While this by no means applies to everyone, it can bestow a cruel bent to the personality. Leos don't like to be blocked or ignored, and because Leo is dependent on continual bolstering from others in the form of outright praise (or, at the very least, respect), Saturn conjunct Leo Mercury can go one of two ways, either making you work harder at your craft or giving you deep fears and insecurities that undermine your already-fragile ego, which creates a constant need for affirmation.

Sagittarius is the bluntest sign in which to have Mercury. Sagittarians seek the truth but also speak the truth, so those with a Sagittarius Mercury are extremely close to the mark when asked for an opinion! Saturn here could be beneficial, making you less likely to offend with your blunt truths, but it blocks your personal search for answers too. You are unlikely to want to discuss any esoteric matters, instead believing in a traditional path that is very straight and narrow—quite the reverse of Mercury in Sagittarius normally.

Air Sign Mercury/Saturn Conjunctions

A Gemini Mercury will be far more grounded and, to a large extent, dulled, by having a conjunction with Saturn. Gemini Mercury's role is to freely move around, making light conversation while imparting facts. The positive here is that notoriously unreliable Gemini might be more likely to turn up for a meeting or date. If you have a Gemini Mercury/Saturn conjunction, you may look to serious conversations when earning your living, working as a news broadcaster rather than a gossip columnist. And when you say something, you might mean it for more than twenty-four hours! Saturn is here to control how Gemini thinks and communicates, bringing some grounding to your ideas and plans.

Libra, whose symbol is the scales of justice because of an ability to make fair and reasoned arguments, will certainly feel the pressure of a heavy Saturn when making decisions. A Libra Mercury/Saturn conjunction will bestow a more negative, pessimistic view of any outcome. Think older parent making a judgement on a wayward child; they are less likely to be lenient if their Libra Mercury is conjunct Saturn.

In a personal sense, if you have a Libra Mercury/Saturn conjunction, it bestows a more negative outlook and a more cautious approach to all decision-making. You may even mistrust your own judgements, believing yourself to be too magnanimous.

How can an Aquarius Mercury be a far-thinking, far-seeing placement when hampered by this most pragmatic planet? If we think of Aquarius as a balloon high in the sky, seeking new heights and new horizons, Saturn will be the one tugging at the end of the string saying, "Come back, you've gone too far!" Depending on how free a thinker you are, this conjunction could be positive or negative. Someone really off-the-wall might benefit from it, but others might not.

Earth Sign Mercury/Saturn Conjunctions

Saturn conjunct an earth sign Mercury will hamper individuals a lot. Earth signs are already cautious. Those with a Taurus Mercury, who are steady enough, will be doubly cautious. There are well-documented difficulties that can occur, though not in every case, when Saturn is conjunct a Taurus Mercury, one being the stammer and/or stutter. Taurus is one of the hardest places to have Mercury, because Mercury is the winged messenger and Taurus is fixed earth—complete opposites. If you have a Taurus Mercury, you likely have trouble expressing yourself. Add Saturn into the mix and it could make you feel socially awkward or shy. Saturn can take a lively, inquiring, optimistic, and cheerful Mercury and douse it with a bucket of cold water, so think of the profound effect it has on those with a Taurus Mercury, already deliberate and careful thinkers.

If you have a Virgo Mercury, you are always tough on yourself. Virgo is dutiful and hard-working, with a serious mindset. Saturn conjunct your Virgo Mercury will make you even more judgemental and cautious. Saturn will perhaps restrain your nit-picking eye for detail, but you are not only a workaholic in the making, but someone with a brutal tongue when roused. Indeed, you are someone who seeks the very best of everything, including yourself—a very hard taskmaster in all ways.

The sign of Capricorn, which Saturn rules, seems to be the one most likely to suffer from various forms of depression, from what was referred to years ago as "the black dog" (lowness of spirits) to seasonal affective disorder to bipolar disorder. In my day, this was common knowledge amongst astrologers based on previous observations over the decades, although it has never been officially proven. But Capricorn's mindset is serious, so if you have a Capricorn Mercury, you strive so hard and work so continuously that it would not be surprising. We all need to let our hair down now and then, but a Saturn conjunction won't allow much room for that. Certainly you are credited with pessimism as one of your traits because of your constant commitment to responsibilities. Failure is the thing most likely to spark negative thoughts, especially if you have worked hard yet achieved little.

Water Sign Mercury/Saturn Conjunctions

Those with a water sign Mercury might be better off when it comes to Saturn conjunctions. People with a Cancer Mercury are usually interested in medical matters as well as subjects that help others. There is a love of history, too, and ancestors. If you have Saturn conjunct your Cancer Mercury, Saturn will give you a more serious bent, with less emotive feelings and more structure. You might end up being a researcher or scientist who looks for medical cures or helps mankind in other ways.

If you have a Scorpio Mercury, you are already driven and secretive. When Saturn is conjunct your Scorpio Mercury, this will give you even greater motivation to seek and find. You are tremendously diligent and serious, with passion, intensity, and the capacity for extremely hard work, although the rewards must be forthcoming. You are never content with what you have achieved, and you are full of fears both real and imaginary (yet always hidden from others). This is a hard aspect to handle, as it makes your thought processes very driven and often dark, yet you have the capacity for great achievement in any field you choose to focus on. You give nothing away and are noncommunicative, which can cause serious issues in your relationships. With Saturn conjunct your Scorpio Mercury, you are someone it's impossible to closely relate to, as you reveal nothing.

A Pisces Mercury already gets bad press because Mercury is in its detriment in Pisces. This is because Mercury's forte is logic, and the sign of Pisces is anything but logical. I often describe having a Pisces Mercury as akin to having your head under the water, and murky water at that. To decide anything at all, intuition has to be accessed, as there are no visible signposts. Saturn conjunct your Pisces Mercury will add some necessary structure and focus, but it will also create even more imaginary fears, which Pisces are so prone to anyway. Saturn is the fear area, so you may have a real problem with communication. Either that or you use the structure and focus Saturn provides as a stepping stone to great works of art, music, or literature.

When Saturn is conjunct any of the signs, it will prevent effusive chatter. It creates a more taciturn frame of mind. As we've seen, while some signs benefit from the structure Saturn provides, it can hamper others.

Relationships could end up being the true victim because those with Saturn conjunct Mercury aren't communicators. How often have you heard someone say, "He/she/they won't talk to me"? It is probably not that they *won't*, but that they *can't*. It's worth noting where Mercury is in the chart of a possible or current partner to be fully prepared.

Like all Saturn positions, there is a reason this inability to freely communicate is in the chart. The sign and house a Saturn conjunction is in will be clues as to how and where blockages are. To find out why, analyse the rest of the chart: the sun's sign and house, the north nodes, and the quadrants.

Venus/Saturn Conjunction

When it comes to Venus, astrology has failed to keep pace with the modern world in many ways. Astrology traditionally links Venus to the female principle because it is deemed a feminine planet, being "watery" and "yielding" in old parlance; all descriptions of how Venus works are based on a purely female principle. It is best to view Venus, therefore, as the planet that reflects the feminine in us all. We all have Venus in our charts, and we all relate to its femininity in some way. For anyone who is seeking love, Venus is the planet to check in a chart, because it shows what we find attractive and alluring.

When Saturn is in conjunction with this gentle, loving planet, it completely overpowers Venus to the extent that love is impossible for the unfortunate person with this pairing. The traditional view of this conjunction is unhappiness in love, and from my experience interpreting charts, this is true; people with Saturn conjunct Venus do have more challenging relationships. But why?

First, let's examine the positive side of this pairing. Venus has the capacity to be unrealistic in its altruistic aims: seeking unconditional love, idealising a partner, expecting sweetness and light forever. Sadly, in the real world these gentle, tender sentiments are often taken advantage of, so Saturn conjunct Venus will confer a more sensible, grounded, realistic view of partnerships. Indeed, this conjunction may incline the individual to seek out a stable, mature, sensible person as a mate. There is a no-nonsense, practical approach to love when Saturn is linked to Venus, which, one would like to think, makes for more realistic relationships.

Venus isn't just about romantic love. The astrological sign it is in shows not only what we find pleasing, but what we look for in a partner too. For example, those with Venus in Capricorn will look for a Capricorn-like partner. They might not seek out a Capricorn, per se, but someone who reflects Capricorn traits: traditional, serious, and hard-working.

To learn what someone deems the true expression of romantic love, look at the sign and house their Venus is in. To further clarify what type of partner they seek, take into account the astrological sign on the descendant (the 7th house). These aspects are a clear guide to the sort of partner someone seeks.

Realistically, some people do cope better with the restraints of Saturn conjunct Venus. If you have Venus in a freer sign, like Gemini, Sagittarius, or Aquarius, you will face tougher challenges, because you need freedom of movement and conversation with lots of people. Saturn linked to Venus will feel far more restrictive for you because it hits at the very core of what makes you happy.

Psychologists have long blamed one's upbringing as the sole reason for an unhappy love life as an adult, though it may actually be due to a Venus/Saturn conjunction. As people are born with this conjunction, this supposes a predisposition to being cool and detached. It's quite possible this conjunction was a pre-life spiritual agreement over which family to be born into. Blaming parents for something their child inherited at birth seems rather unfair!

However, just to muddy the waters, many people with a Venus/Saturn conjunction were abused in some way in childhood, be it emotionally, mentally, physically, or sexually. (This is more prominent in charts where Saturn is in Scorpio—and even then, it is not a given.) Some astrologers claim that it is this harm that stunts the growth of Venusian qualities, because rather than being open to love and trusting and gentle in their affection, individuals expect to be disappointed. Hence, their future partnerships are tainted by their childhood trauma, and the expression of love is one of submission.

Some people who have a Venus/Saturn conjunction actually marry people they don't really like because they have learnt not to love at all; they may take any person who asks because it really doesn't matter to them. There is a cool detachment about those with a Venus/Saturn conjunction that keeps a distance, so even while saying the words "I love you," they don't actually mean them. Or, rather, they mean them as much as they are able to.

Whatever the real reason, whatever the underlying causes—whether a spiritual, cosmic, or karmic lesson, or because of childhood trauma—there is little doubt that when Venus is afflicted by Saturn it can (and often does) create difficulties in one's love life. It is often said that this conjunction causes at least one great sadness in an individual's love life. In general, though, very few people go through life without "the one that got away," so it is debatable how accurate this is. Suffice to say, people with Venus/Saturn conjunct rarely expect an ideal, "happily ever after" marriage, so in many respects this sensible approach saves a lot of heartache. However, it also denies them that close bond that lucky couples achieve.

If you have Saturn conjunct Venus, there is likely a divine discontent that others are happier and loved more deeply than you, as well as a subsequent longing for that same love in your own life. Unless you are spiritually enlightened, you may become trapped by your own experiences of love in childhood and tolerate partners rather than really love them. Our modern, often unrealistic view of relationships is also somewhat to blame, because people expect a happily ever after rather than the true reality of relationships: Relationships are difficult, no matter how much partners love each other.

Whatever the outcome, why is this conjunction in someone's chart in the first place? If you have a Venus/Saturn conjunction, it is important for you to realise that there is a valid reason your relationships are difficult. In previous lives, too much time and attention were given to love, to the detriment of spiritual growth in other areas. In this incarnation, Saturn is stopping you from the tsunami of overwhelming feelings that occur when falling in love. A sensible match found with a sensible approach allows for a partnership *and* the time and space to learn other important cosmic lessons.

To find out what those lessons might be, check the rest of the chart. Life direction can be found by looking at the sun's sign and house, the north nodes, and the quadrant emphasis. If you have this conjunction in your chart, it is highly likely this life is not a personal one, i.e., not about relationships. So, rather than spending your time, energy, and possibly money on an ideal partnership, settle for a partnership that is comfortable and realistic, then focus your energy on your real purpose. Happiness in love is transient and illusive for most people, but modern society has set love on an unrealistic, idealised pedestal. It may be that those with a Venus/Saturn conjunction have a more sensible, objective view of love after all.

Mars/Saturn Conjunction

Neither of these two planets are pussycats. Traditional astrology calls them malefic planets because Mars is the planet of war and Saturn the planet of restriction and delays. Put them together and you have a contradiction of energies, with Mars pushing forward and Saturn holding it back.

Mars rarely acts with forethought. It rules the sign of Aries, which acts first and thinks later; Aries do everything on impulse. So Mars immediately reacts: to defend, to attack, and to move things along. Saturn, on the other hand, pauses action. It encourages forethought, but it is so overly cautious it creates fear. The more we think about things, the more concerned and cautious we become.

This can be considered good or bad. For someone overly eager and thoughtless, a bit of Saturn restraint won't be a bad thing, but generally, Mars represents our motivations in life. We do things because of Mars energy, so when Mars is conjunct Saturn, we will overthink, worry, and fret over outcomes; in the end, fear always holds us back. It is this fear that is Saturn's worst effect.

If you have a Mars/Saturn conjunction, even if you decided to go against all your fears, you would still meet obstacles because that's what Saturn does. It stops us every step of the way and asks again and again, "Are you *sure* this is the right thing to do? What if…?"

Traditional astrology calls Mars an aggressive, masculine planet. Each of us has Mars energy that we access in different ways. Because this conjunction suppresses life force and drive, those who are deeply connected to their Mars energy will be more affected by this conjunction. On the far end of the spectrum, a Mars/Saturn conjunction can lead to cruelty. This cruelty can be physical or mental, with a conjunction in the 8th house particularly mentally cruel.

A Mars/Saturn conjunction in any house that involves another—and many houses involve interactions with others—will indicate a desire to rule, to overcome, to be in control, and to dominate. Traditionally, a Mars/Saturn conjunction is known to cause relationship difficulties with others, from friendship issues to workplace tension to marriage dissolution.

The astrological sign the conjunction is in will give you a lot of information about how it affects you. Some signs are more personal than others. In Leo, for example, this conjunction will hit self-expression, but in a detached sign like Aquarius, it will be less personal and have more to do with friendships.

The house the conjunction is in shows the area of life it will impact. In the 1st house, this conjunction will stop you from pushing yourself forward as you avoid confrontation of every sort. In the 2nd house, it will impact finances; in the 3rd, communication; in the 4th, home and family life; and so on. (The meanings of the houses are listed in the appendix at the back of the book.)

There are positives when Mars and Saturn are together. This conjunction can create good organisational skills and strong willpower. People with this conjunction feel that if they can't control anyone else, at least they can control themselves, and this they certainly do.

My no-go theory suggests that a Mars/Saturn conjunction indicates Mars energy was not handled very successfully in previous lives. It could be that Mars energy was impressed too forcefully on others; there are many examples throughout history of warlike people wreaking havoc. Or this conjunction might simply illustrate that Mars energy was used in an inconsiderate or controlling way in the previous life.

The message with this conjunction is to direct attention away from the self and instead focus on others. If Saturn sits on your Mars, forcing your will on others is to be avoided; that's what Saturn is saying. To more easily understand this conjunction, think of a Saturn in Aries placement. (Aries is the "me" sign, and Mars rules Aries.) Saturn in Aries indicates this life is not about you but about others, and this is also the message of a Mars/Saturn conjunction.

When Mars is conjunct Saturn, carefully analyse the house Mars is in, as this shows the area you should avoid impressing your Mars energy. Then, look at the other indicators of true life direction: the sun, the north nodes, and the quadrant emphasis.

Jupiter/Saturn Conjunction

Often overlooked or dismissed, the planet Jupiter is a vital component in understanding ourselves. In its most simple form, the astrological sign and house Jupiter occupies indicates our area of greatest personal joy. So, how will Saturn affect this beneficial and benign planet?

Saturn is a materialistic planet, whereas Jupiter is one of the mind. Jupiter searches for meaning in life and how to find joy in the mundane, and no planet is more mundane than Saturn. A conjunction between these two will feel like a constant pull of the practical versus the esoteric. Because Saturn is a fear area, instead of embracing wisdom and joy (Jupiter's gifts), there is more of an emphasis on the practical and materialistic aspects of life.

To understand this concept more fully, think of the two astrological signs these planets rule. Saturn rules Capricorn, which is an earth sign and therefore focussed on wealth, status, and achievement in life via sheer staying power and hard work; material gain is sought. Jupiter's sign is Sagittarius, which is a mutable (changeable) sign forever on the go in search of—well, anything and everything, be it new knowledge, new friends, or new adventures. Sagittarius is the sign least likely to be interested in material gain, as Sagittarius has their eyes on the horizons and all the possibilities in the world; their overall aim (whether they realise it or not) is to discover the truth. Sagittarius is the sign accredited with wisdom. Sagittarius is also a fire sign, so it is random and intuitive. Capricorn, as an earth sign, seeks the status quo and looks only to the practical, material world for its pleasures. Jupiter likes to live big without thought of the consequence, whereas Saturn can survive on little if the end result will be worth it. They really are chalk and cheese.

In a Jupiter/Saturn conjunction, Saturn will outweigh Jupiter. Saturn conjunct Jupiter will completely crush the individual's sense of there being a deeper and more profound meaning to life. Saturn takes the joy out of Jupiter. It could evoke a sort of "What's the point?" feeling. A Jupiter/Saturn conjunction can confer a sense of bleakness because Saturn's heavy weight makes it almost impossible for Jupiter to be seen and heard. To better understand how to interpret this conjunction, have a look at the section on Saturn in Sagittarius and/or the 9th house in chapter 3.

While some astrologers overlook this conjunction, believing it does not affect the individual as personally as the more "important" planets, it cannot be ignored. If you have a Jupiter/Saturn conjunction, it affects your life philosophy. Most of your daily actions—indeed, often your whole life—have a purpose based on your individual philosophy. Instead, Saturn forces Jupiter to focus on the practical over the intuitive. Not only that, Saturn takes away Jupiter's natural buoyancy and replaces it with a more severe attitude. This means that instead of the good luck and joy that Jupiter engenders, you will suffer hardship and want, or alternatively, your whole life will become one of keeping the wolf from the door in financial terms. It's hardly any wonder this conjunction causes some people to feel there is no purpose at all.

As with all positions of Saturn, my belief is there is a reason for this. Although it may seem harsh to say someone has to give up their personal philosophy and live a more practical life, a Jupiter/Saturn conjunction denotes that this lifetime is not about you finding your own purpose—it's about what you can do for others. In truth, this conjunction indicates you are already highly enlightened, an old soul. Saturn here is preventing yet another lifetime spent spiritually improving yourself. A pre-life agreement ensured that you entered this life with no distractions from your intended path in the service of mankind. To find out your exact purpose, look to other aspects of your chart: the sun by sign and house, the north nodes by sign and house, and the quadrant emphasis. It's a pretty sure thing this lifetime is about others.

Uranus/Saturn Conjunction

Uranus is an outer planet, sometimes also referred to as a transpersonal planet. What this means is it moves so slowly across the heavens that it is in the same astrological sign for generations of people.

Generally, in a chart, an outer planet is interpreted by the house it is in rather than the sign. The house Uranus is in shows the area of life where the individual will have breakthroughs in outmoded ways of thinking and acting. Uranus rules the sign of Aquarius, and its keywords are creativity, originality, unpredictability, disruptiveness, and restlessness. Aquarius is seen as the sign of both madness and genius because there is a fine line between the two; someone who invents something incredible is a nontraditional thinker. The upheavals Uranus creates usher in new beginnings and innovations in the technical, medical, and scientific fields, and its influence will even affect artistic movements, with art becoming more shocking or unusual.

Saturn next to this unpredictable planet suppresses Uranus's ability to be itself. Saturn likes structure, stability, and the status quo—the exact opposite of Uranus's freedom of thought and action. Basically, Saturn will suppress the wild drive within Uranus so that disruptions are few and far between. If you have this combination of planets (either literally conjunct or in the same house), you tend to adhere to the tried and tested, to the rules and regulations. Now and then, you may experience a moment of wild abandon or a stroke of genius, but it will be quickly suppressed.

According to my no-go theory, Saturn's position is always for a reason. I believe that in this lifetime, you are being advised against allowing any wildness in your personality, particularly in the area of life (the house) these planets are placed. This is to keep you from disrupting what you have built to date. To analyse why you are being asked to follow a traditional path, check out the sun's position by sign and house, the north nodes by sign and house, and the quadrant emphasis.

Neptune/Saturn Conjunction

Neptune is another one of the outer or transpersonal planets that affects whole groups of people due to its slow movement. Like Uranus, it is usually interpreted by house and not sign in a chart. However, the sign Neptune is in can provide clues for finding spiritual oneness, and the house Neptune is in is the area of life we are destined to find spiritual answers/truths.

Neptune has a symbolic association with water: the sea, oceans, streams, and rivers; the subconscious stream of imagination; and what is often called the cosmic ocean. This planet has a mystical feel and deals with love that is totally non-judgemental and accepting—a universal love of mankind. Neptune also rules dreams, ideologies, beliefs, illusions, and self-deception. The downside of Neptune is escapism from the harsh realities of life via drugs and alcohol.

When Saturn is conjunct Neptune, or even in the same house, a battle ensues. Saturn is all about structure, and it is personal, as in "What can I gain? What can I control?" Neptune is about the impersonal, the whole, the letting go of the personal. These two planets are completely at odds with each other when it comes to their feelings and attitudes. A struggle ensues between the need to maintain the personal (Saturn) and the desire to lose it (Neptune). Sometimes this plays out in a form of masochism: giving away the personal to something stronger, a complete self-sacrifice. The problem with Neptune is that any resistance is a passive one, so just like the sign it rules (Pisces), Neptune tends to give in and give way in the face of a stronger, more demanding planet like Saturn. A Neptune/Saturn conjunction will completely overwhelm Neptune.

There are positives to this conjunction. Mainly, Saturn can take Neptune's dreams and make them reality, especially when it comes to music and art. Saturn provides the necessary structure to turn nebulous feelings and imaginings into something concrete.

According to my no-go theory, Saturn is in a position for a particular reason. If you have a Neptune/Saturn conjunction, Saturn is blocking the vague and dreamy feelings that may have held you back from achieving your true potential in previous lives. This conjunction is saying structure is necessary. It's important to check the house the Neptune/Saturn conjunction is in; this is the area Neptune shouldn't be allowed to run unchecked. Also check the position of the sun by sign and house, the north node by sign and house, and the quadrant emphasis to verify your true path in life. It should become obvious why this conjunction is in your chart.

Pluto/Saturn Conjunction

Pluto is one of the outer or transpersonal planets, and it moves very slowly. It takes 248 years for Pluto to orbit the sun, and a lot of time the planet is retrograde (appearing to move backwards). Pluto stays in one sign for between eleven and thirty years, so entire generations have Pluto in the same sign. That's why Pluto is generally interpreted by house.

Pluto rules the sign of Scorpio, and *control* is the key word for Pluto. In a birth chart, the house Pluto is in is the area of life we seek to control. When Saturn is conjunct

Pluto, we have a battle of the giants, with both vying to be in control.

In some ways, Saturn and Pluto are remarkably similar: Saturn forces the individual to confront things in life they'd rather not, and Pluto takes something away to clear the path for the new. Most of us seek to be comfortable, secure, loved, and happy, but both of these planets throw a wrench into the works! Pluto and Saturn force us to experience pain of one kind or another in order to learn and grow, and although we won't like these challenges, we are not physically harmed by them. In fact, we often emerge stronger and with a firmer footing.

When Pluto and Saturn are conjunct, they form a type of obsessiveness, but the true message of this conjunction is not that at all. According to my no-go theory, Saturn is conjunct Pluto to stop its destructive power from spoiling what has been worked so hard for. It seems odd, but Saturn controls Pluto so that Pluto cannot control the individual.

If you have a Pluto/Saturn conjunction, be aware of this obsessive nature while remembering that Saturn is actually the good guy; in past lives, Pluto wreaked havoc on your cosmic path, but this time it won't be allowed to. It's really important to note the house the conjunction is in. Be aware of a desire to force your will in this area, and remember that Saturn is there to stop Pluto from becoming too powerful. One other thing to note is that Pluto likes to work alone, so the house it occupies in a chart is an area you seek to control, *and* you will want to do so alone. For example, if Pluto is in your 10th house of career, you will seek an occupation you can control: owning your own business, being self-employed, or working in isolation.

To better understand the life path to be followed when Saturn and Pluto are conjunct or share the same house, look at the sign and house of the sun, the sign and house of the north nodes, and the quadrant emphasis. It's likely the reason for a Pluto/Saturn conjunction will become clear once you fully understand your chart.

six
The Saturn Return

The Saturn return is when transiting Saturn returns to the same position it is in your natal chart. This first occurs between twenty-seven and thirty-one years of age. Each of us can have up to three Saturn returns in one lifetime because Saturn returns again between fifty-six and sixty years of age, and once more between ages eighty-four and ninety.

Saturn is a slow moving planet—it takes about two and a half years to go through each astrological sign. This is why it is roughly twenty-nine years before Saturn makes a full lap through all of the signs back to where it was when you were born. It's easy to find out when exactly your Saturn return will occur. There are quite a few websites that provide that info. I currently use Astro-Seek.com, which has an online Saturn return calculator.

As soon as Saturn enters the sign it is in in your chart, you may begin to experience the effects of your Saturn return. Because Saturn moves slowly, the events around your Saturn return may be extended over a few years, or there may be one important event that can be easily recalled.

The general consensus is that a Saturn return heralds a life-altering event, be it the birth of a child, a marriage or a serious commitment, a divorce, being fired, a deliberate job or career change, or a complete change in life direction. Sometimes the life-altering event happens unexpectedly; sometimes events happen that force us to make a choice; sometimes we decide to do something that's been on our mind for quite a while.

My belief is that each time Saturn returns to its position at the moment we were born, it is a reminder of our life path (as described in the previous chapters). It's a wakeup call and a shove from the universe.

It has always been accepted that the Saturn return reignites the sign and house your Saturn is in. I now believe it can also trigger anything my new theory links with Saturn (the sun's sign and house and/or the nodes), thus forcing you to rethink your life direction. This means that once you understand what Saturn is saying to you—the area to avoid and the areas you should approach—your

Saturn return will be like a boost that makes sure you are on the correct path.

Alternatively, Saturn may trigger a karmic event that has no connection to your current Saturn position or your nodal axis, or at least no discernible connection. This makes the matter more confusing!

To recap: The Saturn return sometimes triggers the entire pattern Saturn rules (the house Saturn occupies; your nodal axis, regardless of which one it is; and your sun sign position). Other times, it only triggers one aspect. A Saturn return is not a cut-and-dried thing, as it entirely depends on what you have done regarding your cosmic path up to that point. If you are avoiding your cosmic path, you will likely experience events that direct you the right way, but if you've already begun to align with your true path, Saturn return events will be more subtle.

As previously mentioned, sometimes a Saturn return deals with a karmic issue, which means it is very personal, and it may have no apparent connection to your Saturn position. People are usually reluctant to share this information with anyone outside their close circle because of the sensitivity of the issues it covers: relationship issues, not wanting children/wanting children but being unable to, problems within the family or with individual family members, control issues, personal problems at work, and so forth. Karmic issues can cover the whole gamut of life experiences, and neither the event itself nor the eventual outcome can be predicted via the chart.

When it is the nodal axis that is triggered by the Saturn return, it has a more worldly effect, and people *are* willing to share this. Therefore, all the examples in this chapter come from people whose Saturn return affected their nodal axis. Although the following examples make it sound easy, the adjustment from their south to north node often involved real fear, a lot of introspection, and slow but gradual movement. In effect, these situations evolved over a period of time, and they were not easy for the individual.

Whatever happens during your Saturn return, it will be an important thing to note and spend time considering, because the outcome isn't random—it is focussed on you alone. Because we can have up to three Saturn returns during one lifetime, it is not always possible to understand the overall message until much later in life. Each person's chart is highly individual—as is each person—so it cannot be foretold exactly how a Saturn return will affect someone.

Saturn Return Through the Nodal Axes

Sometimes the Saturn return clearly deals with the nodes, which provide clues about our previous lifetime (south node) and where we should be heading in this lifetime (north node). The nodes may have no obvious connection to the position of Saturn in your birth chart, but very often, a Saturn return kick-starts the nodal axis to shove you towards your north node house if you've missed previous opportunities. The following examples will provide more clarity. Check out the appendix in the back of the book if you have questions about the nodes and their meanings.

In this section, the south node position is written first and the north node second. So, if your nodes are in the 3rd/9th houses and your south node is in the 9th, look at the section on 9th/Sagittarius. Remember, the south node is the area and manner of your life in the previous lifetime, so it is your comfort zone. The north node is the complete opposite.

South Node 1st, North Node 7th

If your Saturn return is not linked to a personal karmic event, it may trigger your 1st/7th house nodes. In this case, your Saturn return events will have to do with relationships.

Example

Tom is in his early thirties. He has 1st house south nodes and 7th house north nodes. As a child, he was reserved and had few friends, though this was by choice.

As an adult, when anyone mentioned settling down, Tom would only smile and shake his head. He seemed uninterested in partnerships of any sort—a classic 1st house south node attitude. Tom was perfectly happy with his own company and confident in his own abilities.

When he was twenty-nine and going through his first Saturn return, Tom met someone and fell in love. There were a few rough patches as Tom adjusted to needing someone, but they married a few years later. This broke Tom's past-life south node pattern of independence, and while the partnership will challenge his reluctance to compromise, he has taken the first step towards his north node. This breakthrough shows that a Saturn return can trigger a very straightforward event, especially if it involves the nodal axis.

South Node 2nd, North Node 8th

If your Saturn return is not linked to a personal karmic event, it may trigger your 2nd/8th nodes. If this is the case, it will be the financial arena that comes to the fore.

Example

Joanna has her south node in the 2nd house and her north node in the 8th house, which is advising her that her life path is to learn to graciously accept help from others. She has always been very motivated to work hard and provide for herself, which is indicative of the south node being in the 2nd house: She learnt to be financially independent in her last life, so it is no surprise that Joanna has always been employed—sometimes in more than one job.

At age twenty-eight, at the start of her Saturn return, Joanna had an accident while cycling on a busy road. It left her with many injuries, and it meant she was forced to rely on her family for support (activating her 8th house north node) until she recovered enough to partly rebuild her life. During that period of time, Joanna had to adapt to being cared for. She found it very difficult to accept that she had to be dependent on others, even though they were her family members.

It is still necessary for Joanna to receive some help due to one injury not being completely healed, but she now balances this with working part-time.

South Node 3rd, North Node 9th

If your Saturn return is not linked to a personal karmic event, it may trigger your 3rd/9th nodal axis. If this is the case, it will be the way you communicate and what you communicate that will be impacted.

Example

Faith is a lady in her late sixties who developed a successful media career during her life. She loved the cut and thrust of being at the forefront of what was happening. However, when she retired, Faith felt at a loss.

This sense of loss extended over a period of time Faith remembers as being very frustrating; she felt rootless and useless. Eventually, desperate for some contact with the world, she started to run classes at a local college to teach what she knew. This happened during Faith's second Saturn return.

Despite initially feeling reluctant to be a teacher, Faith found it very fulfilling. Indeed, the local university recently asked her to contribute to a course they have on media studies. This is a classic 9th house north node situation, almost textbook!

South Node 4th, North Node 10th

If your Saturn return is not linked to a personal karmic event, it may trigger your 4th/10th nodal axis. If so, your Saturn return years will have something to do with your career path.

Example

Neil is an intelligent young man in his mid-thirties. When he was younger, he found it hard to settle at any particular career. He flitted from one job to another and generally preferred bar work because of its sociable nature and because he could find work anywhere. Neil felt less restricted because of this freedom. He could (and did) change jobs whenever the mood struck him.

Neil lived at home until he found a partner. Then, they moved in together, and they got married during Neil's first Saturn return, when he was thirty (south node 4th house). A year afterwards, Neil's husband developed an illness that meant he couldn't work, so Neil was required to find a suitable job that could support them both. This event during his Saturn return years triggered his 10th house north nodes and forced him to focus on finding and developing a career.

This didn't happen overnight. In small shifts and changes, Neil tried to make up for the losses in their joint finances. In the end, his current job was offered to him. Although Neil was initially reluctant to have a stable career, he found personal satisfaction in being financially responsible for both himself and his husband.

South Node 5th, North Node 11th

If your Saturn return is not linked to a personal karmic event, it may activate your 5th/11th nodal axis. This will usually involve events that have to do with friendships, both casual and selective.

Example

Marius has 5th house south nodes and is a true life-of-the-party type of person. He is a DJ on his local radio station. However, the station was recently taken over by someone else, and they dropped him, leaving him high and dry during his second Saturn return.

A friend suggested Marius should temporarily DJ at a local hospital, and he found this job fulfilling and rewarding. He regularly went around chatting to people and taking their requests, and Marius became very popular. Now, he occasionally goes to nursing homes and plays the residents music from their youth, something he finds incredibly rewarding due to the warmth and appreciation of the residents. This sort of charitable work (going above and beyond what is expected) with specialist groups is 11th house territory. Marius's example shows that you can take the skills you have and use them in different settings.

South Node 6th, North Node 12th

If your Saturn return is not linked to a personal karmic event, it may trigger your 6th/12th nodal axis. If this is the case, events regarding your cosmic path will occur. If you are living in the past (using the south node tendency to work hard in a hands-on way), you may get a push from the universe that sends you in another direction, or doors that lead to a more introspective life may open for you.

Example

Charlotte, who is now in her fifties, was a dedicated and hard-working teacher and mother of two small children when she had her first Saturn return. Because she was health conscious, Charlotte insisted on cooking all meals from scratch with healthy ingredients. She also refused any help around the house, believing she did a better job. Trying to be all things to all people (6th house south node) resulted in a mental breakdown/exhaustion during her first Saturn return.

After a long period of time to recover, Charlotte stopped teaching and found a less-demanding job. She also employed a cleaner and began buying some ready-made meals. Eventually, she taught the children how to cook so they could help her, and even her husband rustled up the odd meal or two. In all areas, Charlotte tried to relax her iron grip on everything being perfect. To help her mental health, she started meditating and attending yoga classes (12th house activities). Now, twenty years later, Charlotte still meditates and practices yoga, as these activities help her relax and focus on what is really important in life.

South Node 7th, North Node 1st

If your Saturn return is not linked to a personal karmic event, it may activate your 7th/1st nodal axis. In this case, the relationship arena will be affected.

Example

Sarah is a lady in her nineties. Her south node is in the 7th house, north node in the 1st. In her youth, it was expected that Sarah would marry, that she would abide by her husband's wishes, and that she would leave her job once she was married; her husband was expected to support her in those days. This was not a problem for Sarah with 7th house south nodes.

It was only after the death of her husband after more than sixty years of marriage that Sarah finally started to live alone. She was in her eighties at the time. Sarah tells me that she had never lived alone, having stayed at home with her three sisters until she met and married her husband. Starting independent life at her age was a huge challenge, but she had little choice.

Sarah has adapted quite well, and she resists any suggestion she might want to go into sheltered accommodation (apartments for older people that have staff and a call system if they need assistance). She is determined to live independently as long as she possibly can. Sarah's story is a good example of finding our north nodes late in life, as is quite frequently the case.

It sounds like finding her north node area was easy for Sarah, but as with all nodal positions, it certainly wasn't. Sarah suffered greatly as she adapted to being alone for the first time in her life. She had to cope with her personal grief while taking over the finances and the practical side of running a household, all of which was a huge challenge in her older age.

South Node 8th, North Node 2nd

If your Saturn return is not linked to a personal karmic event, it may activate your 2nd/8th nodal axis. If so, something will happen that affects your finances, particularly if you receive benefits from others. You may lose support or, alternatively, ways of supporting yourself may be forthcoming.

Example

Gemma's south node is in the 8th house. Until she was in her late twenties, her partner was willing to fully support her while she cared for their small children. She found this to be a comfortable situation and expected it to continue.

However, Gemma's husband met and fell in love with someone else. Suddenly, at age thirty, during Gemma's first Saturn return, she found herself facing financial responsibility for herself and her children. Thus, Gemma was required to join the workforce, where she initially struggled but eventually found her feet. In fact, she came to enjoy her job and an independent way of living. In retrospect, Gemma wishes she had found a career earlier.

Adjusting to this new way of life happened over a period of three years. According to Gemma, the first year was the hardest because it meant coming to terms with losing her partner so unexpectedly as well as—as she phrased it—"floundering around" while she struggled to adjust to the fact she would need to be the provider. She started with part-time jobs until she adjusted to the working world and gradually gained enough confidence to try her hand at positions that offered more prospects and better pay.

South Node 9th, North Node 3rd

If your Saturn return is not linked to a personal karmic event, it may trigger your 9th/3rd nodal axis. If so, the way you communicate and who you communicate with will be affected.

Example

Anna has always loved literature, writing stories even as a child. However, she went on to study architecture at university, and after receiving her degree, she started her own business with a friend.

At age twenty-nine, Anna wrote a book about her specialist subject. Bear in mind her south nodes are in the 9th house, so it is not surprising her publisher requested she rewrite large parts in order to make it more accessible to the collective; in other words, she was being asked to pass on her wisdom in a way everyone could understand. It took Anna two years to finally complete her project, but she successfully adapted to her 3rd house north node. A second book is planned.

Anna's story is a prime example of the 9th/3rd nodal axis being activated by a Saturn return. She was pushed towards the 3rd house, which involves teaching what you know in a community setting, down in the collective—something those with a 9th house south node may be reluctant to do. It was wise of Anna to rise to the challenge, even in small steps. When the nodal axis is activated, it is the communication of ideas that is important—how one goes about it (art, writing, poetry, singing, acting, teaching) is entirely up to the individual.

South Node 10th, North Node 4th

If your Saturn return is not linked to a personal karmic event, it may trigger your 10th/4th axis of career versus home.

Example

Edward had a career he adored, and one in which he easily rose to the top (south nodes in the 10th house). He began this career during his first Saturn return after trying a few other jobs. He spent most of his life out in the world and enjoyed his status and recognition.

However, during his second Saturn return, Edward's wife had health issues that demanded he be more of a hands-on carer. As she'd been such a staunch supporter of his career and success, he felt honour bound to take a step back from work and care for her himself.

Although it was not an easy process for Edward, he was planning to retire in a few years anyway, which made the transition more mentally acceptable for him. He started by reducing his hours to part-time, and by the time he retired, he had built up enough interest in his home environment to keep him happily occupied. Plus, he grew even closer to his wife as time went on.

Edward now enjoys the freedom to go wherever he wants, whenever he wants. He makes sure he and his wife get as many enjoyable days out as her condition and energy levels allow.

South Node 11th, North Node 5th

If your Saturn return is not linked to a personal karmic event, it may impact your 11th/5th nodal axis. If so, the events that occur will have to do with the groups of people you mix with on a daily basis.

Example

Paula has 11th house south nodes. Despite being incredibly shy and wary of new people, she took a job working in a bar at age twenty-eight. Paula was very reluctant to do this type of work, but she was in a desperate financial position. Once she started, Paula adapted so well that after a few years, she was offered a management position!

Paula still works at the bar and is very happy. Her whole life direction changed during her Saturn return, and although it was initially very scary, Paula is content with where she ended up. She does still maintain a selective friendship group and is still reluctant to attend family events—a good example of keeping a foot in both camps, which is fine.

South Node 12th, North Node 6th

If your Saturn return is not linked to a personal karmic event, it may activate your 12th/6th nodal axis. If so, events may occur that will direct you towards a more practical life of service, as you have already spent one or multiple lives finding spiritual wisdom. It's likely you are an old soul.

Example

Jeanette spent most of her early life studying art. She had a few short stints in the working world while she was a student. Then, Jeanette married and had children, and she chose to stay at home to look after them. She had her own studio at home (12th house south nodes) and used her art as a way to decompress when family life was too demanding.

During her first Saturn return, Jeanette's husband died unexpectedly. Because he was so young, no provision had been made for his family. Initially, Jeanette had huge difficulties accepting she was alone.

Jeanette began to plan what she could do in the working world to support herself and her family. She started teaching art, first to children, but eventually she found the confidence to teach adults too. She also started to take commissions for paintings. As Jeanette still does a lot of work from her home studio, she has kept a foot in both the 12th and 6th houses.

Because of her lowered financial status, Jeanette is now doing far more hands-on work, having taken on the running of the household as well as providing for herself and the children. Her days are busy from dawn to dusk, she says, but she still manages a day alone now and then when the children's grandparents look after them.

seven
Saturn in Synastry

Synastry is the interpretation of two birth charts in relation to each other. The individuals comparing birth charts don't have to be in a romantic relationship; for example, those intending to start a business together would be well advised to check if their charts are in harmony on important matters. Knowing how to read a birth chart would save a lot of heartache in all joint ventures, whether they are platonic or romantic.

Saturn has always been a problem area in synastry. When looking at two charts, all close connections of one's Saturn to other partner's personal planets are problematic in one way or another. However, we all have Saturn somewhere, and humans have been partnering up since time immemorial, so it isn't necessarily a disaster waiting to happen.

Many partners have Saturn in a position that doesn't impact a planet but will still affect the partner's area of life (house). The only time a partner's Saturn won't have such an impact is if both Saturns are in the same house. For example, I know a couple who both have 3rd house Saturns; this means they will both be avoiding the same area. Lots of couples have Saturn in the same sign, as Saturn stays in one sign for nearly three years, but it's less likely for their Saturns to be in the same house.

My new no-go theory of Saturn makes little difference to how we interpret it in synastry. Saturn is Saturn. If it falls in a house, it will still suppress that area in a partner's chart. However, enlightenment regarding Saturn can certainly be beneficial. If each person understands the other's Saturn position, it will help enormously.

Assuming that Saturn's position is a pre-life decision, cosmic lessons during this lifetime may include interacting with someone via our Saturn position. For example, if your partner's Saturn is conjunct your sun (a conjunction that has always been viewed as very difficult), there may be pre-decided obligations between the two of you. This position can mean both partners provide support and structure to the other, perhaps one emotionally and the other financially; there will be a sense of obligation and a feeling that the obligation cannot be sidestepped. There is one easy way to determine whether or not a relationship is fated (meant to be for karmic or cosmic purposes): If a relationship survives despite an apparently difficult aspect pattern, the couple has issues to resolve around past lives. These couples will certainly face challenges, but they will work together to overcome them, and in doing so they will form a deep and lasting bond.

When you enter a relationship of any sort, Saturn is an important planet to check. In what area of life will you be struggling to understand each other's stance? Is their Saturn affecting one of your personal planets, and if so, is it something you can tolerate and accept? Be aware that the house Saturn occupies in your partner's chart is the area they are not supposed to go. Make sure you are not pushing them in a direction they are meant to avoid. Equally, make your partner aware of your Saturn area and where you must not go.

In a romantic relationship, it is easy to overlook differences in the first flush of love, but eventually they all hit home. The problem areas for couples are often finances and whether or not they want children, so the 2nd and 5th houses are particular areas to note. If starting a business with someone, the 2nd house (finances) and the 10th house are the most important areas to look at. Platonic relationships can usually weather all sorts of problems because there is a less intense reliance on each other, and quite frankly, if Saturn was causing a problem, it's unlikely individuals would be friends anyway.

When comparing two charts, always remember that this works both ways: Your partner's Saturn placement will affect you, and your Saturn will affect your partner, depending on which planet and/or house it has contact with. After looking into your synastry with another, try and be aware if you are deliberately or unintentionally suppressing one of your partner's planets or an area of life. With any Saturn contact, it is important to resist expressing disapproval. To maintain a good relationship, it is necessary to give and take; allow a partner's character to be expressed the way they desire.

To determine your synastry with a partner, first determine your own Saturn position. To do this involves looking at the sign your Saturn occupies. Note the exact degree of your Saturn. Then, determine which house of your partner's chart that sign is in. Then, plot your Saturn to the degree. For example, my Saturn is in Scorpio, and in my husband's chart, the sign of Scorpio is in his 10th house. Thus, my Saturn will be in his 10th house.

Once you have plotted your partner's Saturn in your chart, do the reverse. Find out the sign your partner's Saturn is in, determine the degree, and place it in your own chart. After the initial look at Saturn according to sign, it is the house that is relevant—the sign is used simply to ascertain the planet's position in each other's chart.

Saturn's Effect on the Planets in Synastry

This section will explain how links between one partner's planet and the other partner's Saturn will impact the relationship. Once you know where Saturn is in each other's chart, you can determine whether or not there are any aspect patterns between planets.

First, find out where exactly your Saturn is in your partner's chart. Then, see if Saturn is within 5 degrees of any of your partner's planets. If the answer is yes, the two planets form a conjunction. Determine if there are any other aspects between Saturn and your partner's planets, then read the appropriate section(s) below.

The Conjunction

This is the most difficult aspect to have. It is when Saturn is close (within 5 degrees) to a planet in the partner's chart. When Saturn is conjunct another planet, it will try to completely suppress the other planet. It is particularly important to know that although this sounds very negative (and indeed can be felt negatively), if one or both partners understand what is going on and make allowances, long relationships can ensue. Awareness and understanding are key.

The Sextile and Trine

These aspects are easier to navigate. Depending on the site you are using, they are usually shown as blue lines between Saturn and another planet. Sextile and trine aspects are a beneficial link because of the wise advice/structure the Saturn partner will offer.

The Semi-Sextile and Quincunx

On the site I use, these are shown as green aspect lines between Saturn and another planet. The semi-sextile and quincunx are ambiguous links that create confusion. If your partner's Saturn is quincunx any of your planets, it will make you question yourself. *Maybe the Saturn partner is right?* you'll wonder. These aspects create self-doubt.

The Square and Opposition

The square and opposition are not particularly good aspects. They are often depicted as red lines. Although squares and oppositions are preferable to an actual conjunction (Saturn is always better at a distance; sitting right on top of planet gives it no room to breathe), these are tense links.

The square is indicative of arguments. For example, if your partner's Saturn is square your Mercury, they may ridicule or mock the way you speak or what you say; because your Mercury does have some breathing space (being three astrological signs apart), you will verbally fight back. Alternatively, the Saturn partner may trigger you to work harder or push yourself more, which could be a positive.

The opposition is like having someone pulling you back all the time, creating doubts. If your partner's Saturn is in opposition to one of your planets, the Saturn partner's voice may keep popping up as you go about your life, planting doubts like "Are you sure? Maybe it's best not to." This aspect pattern won't stop you so much as make you question everything you do.

Saturn's Effect on the Planets

In the previous section, we looked at the possible aspects between Saturn and a partner's planets. In this section, I will go into more detail about each planet and the effect Saturn has on it when they form an aspect pattern. In particular, this section refers to the conjunction. Saturn's effects will still be felt in other negative aspects, such as the square and opposition, though to a lesser degree.

As previously mentioned, some of the more pleasant aspect links (semi-sextile and trine) will still have an influence, but that influence will come in the form of wise advice.

Saturn/Sun

Saturn will affect the sun's ability to shine, but this can work if the sun person needs some self-discipline. Otherwise, it's likely to be a non-starter, as the sun person will feel their Saturn partner restricts their ability to be themselves.

However, if the sun person is looking for someone stronger and wiser who can advise them, guide them, or provide structure in their life, this link could help the relationship stand the test of time. At times of crisis in someone's life, their sun is more likely to be drawn to a strong Saturn link due to the stability and maturity the Saturn person offers.

Saturn/Moon

Saturn will suppress the emotions of the moon person and be critical of their emotional stance. This is a pairing that is unlikely to last, as we all need to be understood. This is a very negative position for Saturn, with no redeeming features. Best avoided.

Saturn/Mercury

Saturn may criticise or undermine the way the Mercury person communicates, or even tell them to be quiet! Sometimes the Saturn person won't even listen. This doesn't necessarily mean disaster; the Saturn person thinks differ-ently, that's all, and they express it as a form of disapproval. Discussion about this may help resolve tensions.

Saturn/Venus

Saturn will suppress the naturally loving side of the Venus person, making them believe they are overly romantic or too needy. It may be that they are, or it may be that the Saturn person is too cool for the Venus person. Counsel-ling and/or a frank discussion (if possible) may clear up misunderstandings.

Saturn/Mars

Saturn will suppress Mars's drive by belittling, undermin-ing, or undervaluing the Mars person's aims in life. Alter-natively, if the Mars person has difficulty deciding what to do, they may appreciate the Saturn person's wise advice and support.

Saturn/Jupiter

Saturn will suppress the sense of joy in the Jupiter per-son. This is one of the most unhappy pairings for partners to have. It is unlikely any discussions or counselling will resolve this. Truthfully, relationships where one person makes the other feel unhappy are unlikely to progress.

Saturn/Saturn

A Saturn/Saturn conjunction is a beneficial aspect. If both Saturns are in the same house, each partner is avoiding/suppressing the same thing. That makes life easier!

When it's another aspect, particularly the opposition, the partnership will struggle. One partner will be significantly older than the other, so they will have different ways of doing things.[5] Of course, it is possible to overcome all obstacles with wisdom and determination, but it certainly won't be easy.

The square will also be a challenging aspect, and it is best avoided. The more harmonious links—the sextile and trine—will work fine as long as each partner understands the other's Saturn lessons.

Saturn/Uranus

Saturn will add common sense and logic, halting Uranus's wilder episodes—not necessarily a bad thing. Saturn rules Capricorn, which is a traditional, conservative sign, so it doesn't understand Uranus's need to be different simply for the sake of it. The Saturn partner will not like the Uranus person rocking the boat when everything is stable, so

5. Saturn takes approximately twenty-eight to twenty-nine years to do a complete circle of the chart through all the signs, so if Saturns are in an opposition (separated by half the chart), this indicates a fourteen-year age gap.

the Uranus partner may find their individuality being un-
dermined.

Saturn/Neptune

Saturn may not understand the Neptune person's dreams
and ideals, but they may be able to offer concrete advice
on how to make money from some of their Neptune partner's creative projects.

Saturn/Pluto

Two giants go head to head. Who will win? Pluto for sure,
though it will be a battle. This is all about control in a certain area, and as Saturn rules Capricorn and Pluto rules
Scorpio, the battle could be quite erotic, or brutal at times.
Not a relaxing partnership by any means!

Saturn/North Nodes

People don't really want to move towards the house/area
their north nodes are in. When Saturn and the north
node are conjunct, Saturn will want to block that area as
well, meaning the Saturn person will hamper their partner's spiritual growth. This is unlikely to be a lasting partnership because we must (and do) end up accessing parts
of our north node house.

Saturn's Effect in the Houses

To recap, in synastry, your partner's Saturn will fall in one area of life (house) in your chart. To find out exactly where their Saturn is in your chart (and vice versa), check what astrological sign your partner's Saturn is in, and note the exact degree. You can look at the list of planets that often accompanies internet charts to locate Saturn's exact position. Then, find that sign in your own chart and plot that exact degree. For example, if your partner has Saturn in Aries at twenty degrees, find twenty degrees Aries in your own chart, and that's where their Saturn will fall.

It is very rare to find two people with Saturn at the same degree and in the same sign and house unless they were born at around the same time, on the same day, in the same year. If this happens, neither will be affected by the other's Saturn, as their own Saturn will be a sufficient deterrent from that area. Both will have similar feelings about that area of life, and neither will be interested in that house at all. However, two partners with the same Saturn placement will most likely have completely different spiritual paths in life depending on their sun, north node, and quadrant positions.

In most cases, there will be areas of life each of you must access alone. Your partner's Saturn may be in a house that is important to you. For example, their Saturn could be in your 5th house, but maybe you have a 5th house sun and enjoy performing at a local theatre. Your Saturn partner might initially ask you to take a step back from the theatre. However, once you explain that it is important to you, they might relent but still have no interest in attending your plays. Try not to take this personally. In other words, make allowances. The relationship has a better chance of long-term survival if you allow each other these personal freedoms, along with the trust and faith that goes along with them.

Although Saturn contacts are considered negative, Saturn can also offer wise advice and caution. In many instances, relationships where partners have Saturn contact can survive, especially when there is a lot of love between the couple and/or other positive chart aspects. Often, the Saturn partner is not deliberately being controlling or undermining, but it is felt by their partner that they are. Talking these things through can resolve a lot of the difficulties; partners should point out things that are uncomfortable so they can be discussed and resolved. After all, they wouldn't be together in the first place if there wasn't a desire to be together.

1st House

When your partner's Saturn falls in your 1st house, it could hamper your ability to be who you really are. Your Saturn partner may not actually say anything, but you could feel unable to be truly yourself. Or they might make comments about your appearance, clothes, etc. Because Saturn is quite conservative, these comments could be a request to be more modest in your attire or manners.

2nd House

When your partner's Saturn falls in your 2nd house, the Saturn partner could drain your resources, undermine your earning ability, or criticise the way you work or the job you do; perhaps all of the above. This is a difficult house to have a partner's Saturn in. As a couple, you are unlikely to accumulate wealth or property. This is a relationship best avoided unless the Saturn partner is offering wise advice regarding investments/money/property.

3rd House

When your partner's Saturn falls in your 3rd house, the Saturn partner may stop you from communicating effectively. It's likely you'll feel unable to speak your mind. Alternatively, your Saturn partner may have a request about the way you communicate. For example, they could ask you to stop using social media so much, especially when you are out together. While this is a valid request, it would still be felt as a restriction on how and when you communicate.

4th House

Saturn is notoriously difficult in the area of home and family. When your partner's Saturn falls in your 4th house, the Saturn partner could make home a cold, unfeeling place because of a lack of interest, a lack of desire to settle down and have a family, or an inability to be warm and loving. The Saturn person won't be interested in the aspects of family life that most people are, such as going to a family gathering. In fact, the Saturn partner is unlikely to actively participate in family activities of any sort, or they will do so very reluctantly.

Platonic relationships experience the same effects if the pair live together. The Saturn person won't be interested in taking on their share of chores/responsibilities. Additionally, any aspect that involves family will be avoided by the Saturn person.

5th House

When your partner's Saturn falls in your 5th house, their Saturn could suppress your creative side in some way. It's also possible that they will either not want children or be unable to have them. They likely won't enjoy the same things you do, but hopefully talking things through will alleviate some of the possible difficulties—you can both enjoy your creative activities alone or with others of like mind.

6th House

When your partner's Saturn falls in your 6th house, the Saturn partner could be disinterested in aspects of a health, nutrition, or fitness regime that you follow. It's likely they won't be as keen to keep fit. Alternatively, they could be ultra-fit and encourage you to follow suit.

As this is the house of serving others, the Saturn partner may not want you to do so much for others. This desire could be out of genuine concern.

All of these issues can be resolved with discussion.

7th House

When your partner's Saturn falls in your 7th house, the Saturn partner could become a burden to you in some way. Perhaps they are older and will require care in the future, or they will become ill, or they will lose their job; there are numerous scenarios that could occur, and many of them are out of anyone's control.

Alternatively, it may be that the Saturn partner is practical and sensible about love rather than romantic. Saturn does guarantee longevity in a partnership, so this relationship can stand the test of time. There is a bond of responsibility when Saturn is in the 7th, and while difficult, couples rarely actually leave the relationship despite the hardships. This placement can indicate either a cosmic lesson or a karmic debt of some sort.

8th House

The 8th house covers many aspects: psychology, death, sexuality, and what belongs to other people, such as money and property. For example, if your partner's Saturn falls in your 8th house, the Saturn partner is unlikely to provide for you after their death, quite possibly because they will be unable to. Alternatively, the Saturn partner may use subtle psychological manipulation to get you to do what they want. The 8th house is ruled by Scorpio, and there may be undertones of "transactions" about the relationship.

There will be a lot of challenges around money, sex, and psychological interplay, but this certainly won't be a boring relationship. And, if both partners are up for the challenge, it could be quite sexy. This relationship certainly can stand the test of time.

9th House

When your partner's Saturn falls in your 9th house, they may not want to go abroad or travel to foreign places, or they may not want to accompany you on your travels. There could be diverging interests in esoteric matters—they might not believe what you believe. But with tolerance and understanding, there is no reason why these issues can't be resolved or simply accepted.

10th House

When your partner's Saturn falls in your 10th house, the Saturn partner will likely encourage you to have a more stable, financially rewarding job. This may sound like they are criticising what you do for a living, but Saturn often offers wise advice, so maybe you should think about it!

Alternatively, the Saturn partner may not be interested in your career, but that could be because it is out of their sphere of interest.

11th House

When your partner's Saturn falls in your 11th house, it is your chosen friendships and ideals that the Saturn partner may not be happy about. It's unlikely they will be interested in the clubs and groups you join. In fact, they may advise against them, perhaps astutely recognising your friends/groups are not true and reliable. Their advice could be beneficial.

12th House

When your partner's Saturn falls in your 12th house, your spiritual beliefs and any religious leanings will be at odds with your Saturn partner's, who won't understand them or share the same feelings. This does not necessarily spell disaster, as our personal beliefs do not have to be shared with our partner. After all, people of different belief systems frequently marry.

After you have checked where your partner's Saturn falls in your chart, reverse the process and check where your Saturn falls in your partner's chart. Then, read the appropriate section to see how you may be restricting them.

Conclusion

The easiest way to understand Saturn's role is to think of it like a road block in a certain area of life—a "No Entry" sign. That is why all efforts to move towards the area of life Saturn occupies are constantly blocked. The universe is trying to tell you something, so you need to listen to it. It could be that in past lives, you already dealt with that area of life, or maybe being drawn down that path would dilute your real purpose.

On the earthly plane, we have no clear picture of the bigger plan for our souls; all we can do is use our birth chart as our map and guide while trusting that the universe has our back. We all have dreams, but some of them are just not going to be possible in this life; knowing that can leave us with a sense of certainty and understanding.

When I was studying astrology, I was taught that if one was enlightened enough, they could "rise above" their chart, but in all honesty, I've never encountered that. All of us work with the energies we were gifted in our chart, and we all—in one way or another—end up fulfilling our destiny as described there. This leads me to believe that when it comes to our life path, free will and free choice are an illusion; life takes us where we are meant to be.

It seems that Saturn isn't the bad guy he has always been painted as after all. He is one of the good guys who is showing us our true path and purpose! Let's stop hating Saturn and instead start loving him for showing us the blocked areas, and for the unique roadmap he is giving us towards our own personal enlightenment and learning.

appendix
Astrology Basics

A birth chart is a picture of the sky the moment you took your first breath. It shows the exact planetary placements you were born under. A birth chart is a circle with you at the centre. Imagine looking up from that centre, and this is the alignment of the astrological signs, planets, and houses at your moment of birth.

As the sky looks different from moment to moment and place to place, it is important to know the exact time and place you were born. It's easy to see your birth chart; just go to a website that offers a free chart; type in your time, date, and place of birth; and print your chart out or take a screenshot.

Everything that you see in a birth chart means something about who you are and how you act, but it also covers important information about your destiny and life purpose. A birth chart seems complicated when you first look at it, but it is like an onion, with each layer revealing a deeper meaning. The easiest way of describing a birth chart is to say that it is a map of your life.

How Does Astrology Work?

The exact origins of astrology are obscured by time, and there are contradictory views. This isn't the place to discuss this point, but do look online if you want to know more. What we know for sure is that ancient astrologers divided the sky into the twelve astrological signs of Aries, Taurus, Gemini, Cancer, Leo, Virgo, Libra, Scorpio, Sagittarius, Capricorn, Aquarius, and Pisces, based on constellations. These are the symbols that go around the whole chart circle counterclockwise, and it's likely you recognise at least some of them.

Then, the sky was divided into twelve houses, which are areas of life. The houses cover every aspect of human life. For example, the sun will be in an astrological sign, but it will also be in a house, and the house it is in will show an astrologer in what area of life you express your sun's energy and drive.

The houses are not always easy to see. They are usually shown by small lines coming out from the astrological signs. Usually these dividing lines are black, but sometimes four important lines are marked in red: on the far left, the rising sign (still written as AC because it was previously referred to as the *ascendant*); at the bottom, the IC (a Latin phrase, *Imum Coeli*, which means "bottom of the sky"); the DC on the far right, which stands for the *descendant* and highlights the ways we interact with other people; and at the top, the MC, the *midheaven*, which is the highest point we can achieve in life, usually via our career. In some online charts, the houses are denoted by very small numbers near the sign's symbol.

The next thing to look for in a birth chart are the planets. These are the ten planets that are in fairly close proximity to Earth. They are the sun, moon, Mercury, Venus, Mars, Jupiter, Saturn, Uranus, Neptune, and Pluto. It's likely some of the symbols for the planets are recognisable to you—the moon in particular. Each planet has its own unique purpose and energy. Because of this mapping of the sky, each planet will fall in one of the astrological signs and in a house. This information will show an astrologer how that planet's energies are used and expressed.

There is another symbol in the chart that looks a bit like a headset. These are the north nodes, and they are your marker to this life's cosmic purpose.

The colourful lines you see spanning the chart are aspect lines and show links between planetary energies; they indicate if the planets are working in harmony or if their energies are in opposition, causing tension. The balance of coloured lines is also important; is one colour more dominant than the others?

Finally, there are the quadrants. Divide the chart in half and then into quarters in your mind. Planets in the halves—the whole left side, the whole right side, the top section, or the bottom section—tell an astrologer something, as do planet groupings in the four quadrants.

Interpreting a chart involves analysing and assessing all this information: astrological sign characteristics, planet energies, houses, aspect lines, and quadrant information.

The Zodiac Signs: Motivations and Elements

Each of the twelve zodiac signs has a unique energy and motivation. The easiest way to understand yours is through its elemental information. Is it cardinal, fixed, or mutable, and is it a fire, earth, air, or water sign? Knowing these two things will give you a really good idea of how a sign works.

The Motivations

Cardinal signs are capable, bold, and driven. They can pick themselves up after disasters.

Fixed signs are stable, reliable, and stubborn. They dislike change, and they have difficulty adapting to new circumstances.

Mutable signs are flexible and adaptable, so they handle life's fluctuations well, but they are hard to pin down.

The Elements

Fire signs are bold, adventurous, impatient, and driven.

Earth signs are stable, seek security, and prefer the status quo.

Air signs use their minds. Their motivation is to communicate, study, research, and teach.

Water signs are the feeling signs. They are sensitive, empathic, and caring.

Motivation and Element Combinations

Find out the element and motivation of your sun sign, then expand on what you've learned in the previous sections. Your sun sign's element and motivation will show how you use your energy in life.

- Aries is cardinal fire.
- Taurus is fixed earth.
- Gemini is mutable air.
- Cancer is cardinal water.
- Leo is fixed fire.

- Virgo is mutable earth.
- Libra is cardinal air.
- Scorpio is fixed water.
- Sagittarius is mutable fire.
- Capricorn is cardinal earth.
- Aquarius is fixed air.
- Pisces is mutable water.

Sun Signs

The sun is the most important planet in your birth chart, and the astrological sign it is in at your birth describes who you really are. It's how you express your identity and individuality.

The sun is the only planet we can assign dates to because it takes one year for the earth to circle the sun; the other planets move faster or slower and so are impossible to assign exact dates to. Sometimes, though, there is a difference of a day or two in the yearly sun sign dates because while the sun's orbit is a circle of 360 degrees, there are 365 days in a year. This is another reason that your time of birth needs to be accurate. Some people think they are "on the cusp" of two signs, meaning they are a bit of both signs, but your time of birth will tell you exactly which sign you really are.

Aries (March 21–April 19) is a cardinal fire sign. Aries suns are driven, capable, impatient, and bold. They can cope with life's ups and downs and enjoy starting new things. Their symbol is the ram because they face life head-on and batter down opposition rather than avoid it.

Taurus (April 20–May 20) is a fixed earth sign. Taurus suns are the most stable sign of the zodiac. They dislike change of any sort, and they stick to every choice they make, from their life partner to their house. They have trouble adapting to unexpected circumstances. Their symbol is the bull because of this fixity.

Gemini (May 21–June 21) is a mutable air sign. Gemini is the most difficult sign to pin down. They thrive on communication, change, and variety, so they find it hard to stay put in one place, with one partner, or in one job. Their symbol is the twins, which shows their restless, changeable nature. They can say something one day and espouse the opposite view the next.

Cancer (June 22–July 22) is a cardinal water sign. Cancer suns are sensitive and caring, but they are stronger than they look. Being a cardinal sign, they can cope with life's ups and downs. Their symbol is the crab, which shows how vulnerable they are as well as how they protect themselves with their hard outer shell.

Leo (July 23–August 22) is a fixed fire sign. They are warm, generous, and loyal, but they expect thanks for the considerable amount they do for others. This is shown by their symbol, the lion, who looks after their pride but expects to be number one.

Virgo (August 23–September 22) is a mutable earth sign. Virgo suns are hard-working and dutiful but have high and exacting standards. Their symbol is the earth maiden who attends to the practical matters of life, which makes them really good with details.

Libra (September 23–October 23) is a cardinal air sign. Libra suns are logical, balanced, and fair. The scales are their symbol, which shows how they use their mind to achieve harmony. They seek to keep everyone happy with their reasoned judgements.

Scorpio (October 24–November 21) is a fixed water sign. Scorpio is famed for its passion and intensity. Water signs are deeply sensitive and emotional, and because of its fixity, Scorpio is unable to let slights go. Scorpio's symbol is the scorpion because they are self-protective and will seek revenge on anyone who hurts them or their loved ones.

Sagittarius (November 22–December 21) is a mutable fire sign, so Sagittarius suns are restless and changeable, forever on the move. Their symbol is the archer. Wherever the arrow lands, Sagittarius will go in search of something new. Truth is important to them.

Capricorn (December 22–January 19) is a cardinal earth sign. Capricorn suns focus on working hard and building security. They want to make their mark on the world, so they pursue money, real estate, and status. Their symbol is the goat, which shows their determination to reach the pinnacle of life, even if it is a slow ascent.

Aquarius (January 20–February 18) is a fixed air sign. They are original and unpredictable, and their fixity shows in their determination to be themselves. They don't adapt to others—they go their own way. Their symbol is the water carrier, which reflects their humanitarian, nonjudgemental drive.

Pisces (February 19–March 20) is a mutable water sign. Pisces suns are extremely sensitive and compassionate, but because they are mutable, they are impossible to pin down; they slip away to calm waters when life gets tough. Their symbol shows two fish swimming in opposite directions, which reflects their inability to make decisions.

The Houses

Houses are areas of life. A birth chart is divided into twelve houses. When a planet falls in a particular house, its energies are interpreted in context of the meaning of the house.

The 1st house is the ascendant/rising sign and reflects how we wish to be perceived; it's what people see/feel the first time they meet us. The houses go in sequence, starting with the rising sign, and move counterclockwise around the chart.

1. The rising sign; how we want others to see us; our sun sign in the previous life
2. Money and possessions
3. Communication; early education; siblings; neighbours; short journeys
4. Home and family
5. Creativity, fertility, and self-expression
6. Work, health, and service to others
7. Marriage and long-term partnerships
8. Sex; death; psychology; what other people own and value
9. Philosophy, higher learning, and long-distance travel
10. Career and status
11. Friendships, groups, and shared ideals
12. The hidden self and spiritual beliefs

The Planets

The ten astrological planets are the sun, moon, Mercury, Venus, Mars, Jupiter, Saturn, Uranus, Neptune, and Pluto. They each reflect different facets of our personality.

The first seven are called *personal planets* because these are used in everyday life. The three outer planets of Uranus, Neptune, and Pluto are called *transpersonal planets* or *outer planets*. They move very slowly across the sky, and therefore whole generations of people have them in the same sign (though not necessarily in the same house).

- **Sun:** The sun's position in the chart, by astrological sign and house, shows our main focus in life and where we get our sense of identity.
- **Moon:** The moon's position, by sign and house, shows how we respond emotionally to people, objects, and places.
- **Mercury:** This planet's position explains how we learn, teach, and communicate.
- **Venus:** The position of Venus shows how we love and what brings us personal contentment.
- **Mars:** The position of Mars, by sign and house, shows what drives us in life.
- **Jupiter:** Where Jupiter falls is an area of wisdom, abundance, and pleasure.
- **Saturn:** Traditionally, Saturn's sign and house show the difficulties we will face in life. My new no-go theory explains why this is the place we are blocked from going.

- **Uranus:** The position of Uranus shows the area of life sudden, unexpected disruption is likely to occur.

- **Neptune:** Its position shows the area of life where confusion and deception will abound.

- **Pluto:** Pluto represents the area of life we want to control.

The outer planets in conjunction with (right next to) other planets—especially the personal ones—can radically affect them, making them more disruptive and unpredictable (Uranus), vague (Neptune), or controlling (Pluto).

The south node is not a planet, but a past-life marker. The north node shows us our cosmic path in this life. Technically, the north node is a mathematical point relating to the positions of the sun, moon, and Earth at the moment of birth; it is the point at which the moon's orbit intersected the plane of the ecliptic.

House and Sign Rulers

Each house relates to an astrological sign, and each astrological sign has a planet assigned to it. This planet is the ruler of both the sign and the house. The signs and houses go in sequence, from Aries to Pisces, counterclockwise from the 1st house. So, the 1st house is ruled by Aries, the 2nd house by Taurus, the 3rd by Gemini, and so forth.

Often, beginners get confused by this concept, but a ruler is just an easy way of remembering what the house is all about. For example, Gemini is the 3rd sign, and therefore it rules the 3rd house, which is itself ruled by the planet Mercury. Mercury is the winged messenger of Greek and Roman myth, also referred to as Hermes. This sign and house is therefore about communication, friends, neighbours, and the local community. Other planets in this sign (Gemini) and this house (the 3rd) will want to express themselves in a Gemini way by teaching, communicating, and being active in the community, regardless of what astrological sign is in the 3rd house in an individual's chart.

For example, if a chart has the sign of Scorpio in the 3rd house, the individual will approach teaching and learning in a Scorpio way: with intensity and purpose. They will also be reserved in the way they communicate, because Scorpios are not communicative. If, however, Capricorn is in the 3rd house, individuals will want to study traditional subjects or teach the way things have always been done; they will express conservative views. On the other hand, if Aquarius is the sign in the 3rd house, they will prefer unusual subjects. If the individual is a teacher, they will teach in a completely different way or find new ways of teaching. They will also enjoy shocking people by expressing different and unusual views. And so on.

- Aries rules the 1st house and is ruled by Mars.
- Taurus rules the 2nd house and is ruled by Venus.
- Gemini rules the 3rd house and is ruled by Mercury.
- Cancer rules the 4th house and is ruled by the moon.
- Leo rules the 5th house and its ruled by the sun.
- Virgo rules the 6th house and is ruled by Mercury.
- Libra rules the 7th house and is ruled by Venus.
- Scorpio rules the 8th house and is ruled by Pluto.
- Sagittarius rules the 9th house and is ruled by Jupiter.
- Capricorn rules the 10th house and is ruled by Saturn.
- Aquarius rules the 11th house and is ruled by Uranus.
- Pisces rules the 12th house and is ruled by Neptune.

Note that Venus rules two signs and houses, as does Mercury. In past times, until the more recent discoveries of Uranus, Neptune, and Pluto, other signs shared a ruler too: Saturn rules Capricorn, but it also ruled Aquarius until Uranus was discovered in 1781. Jupiter ruled Pisces as well as Sagittarius until Neptune came to light in 1846. Mars, the ruler of Aries, also ruled Scorpio until Pluto's discovery in 1930. This suggests there are two more planets yet to be discovered so that each astrological sign would have its own ruling planet.

Aspects

Aspects are links between planets. Very close aspects mean the planet's energies work together. Aspects will show up as lines in the middle of a birth chart, and they will be various colours. Every computer site does the colours a bit differently, though I've provided the standard colours used for these lines.

The main aspects are:

- **Conjunction:** Planets right next to, or within a few degrees of, each other. Usually, the colour orange is used to show a conjunction.
- **Semi-Sextile:** A short line 30 degrees between planets that shows a natural and easy working between the planets involved. No effort is required; it is an innate ability. Often, this line is depicted as green.

- **Sextile:** An easy link between planets 60 degrees apart. Usually shown as a short blue line.
- **Square:** A short line 90 degrees between planets that shows an energetic, working energy between them that can cause friction. This line is typically red in a birth chart.
- **Trine:** An aspect that is 120 degrees between planets. This is drawn as a long blue line and reflects a harmonious link between the planets involved.
- **Quincunx:** A long green line 150 degrees between planets that shows a searching quality. Often, there is a divine discontent with this—there is knowledge of something more but an inability to find it, which leads to a constant, vague discontent.
- **Opposition:** A long line (often red) that spans the whole chart, 180 degrees apart. This line indicates a tension between two planets that is rarely resolved. In particular, when the sun and moon are in opposition, this can cause lifelong difficulties.

Aspect Patterns

Sometimes the aspect lines form patterns, mostly triangles in the various colours, but there are other, less-obvious patterns that astrologers interpret. The patterns are made up of the red, green, and blue aspect lines, and the colour of the pattern is very important.

Red lines forming patterns (square and opposition) often cause tension, though the square can be energising.

Blue lines forming patterns (trine and sextile) are innate talents and abilities that come naturally and don't have to be worked at.

Green lines need other coloured lines to form a pattern (quincunx and semi-sextile). Green patterns show someone is a thoughtful person who questions things.

The only aspect pattern referred to in this book is the efficiency triangle, sometimes called a T-square. It is an all-red triangle that shows a lot of energy expended into the planet and house at the apex of the triangle.

The Quadrants

In this book, the quadrants are particularly important, showing where to direct your energy in life via the sun and north nodes.

To find the quadrants in a chart, draw an imaginary line from the MC (midheaven) at the top of the chart down to the IC (roots) at the bottom of the chart. Then draw another line from the AC (ascendant) across to the DC (descendant). This will cut the chart into four sections, which we call the quadrants.

The Halves/Sides

The chart can be looked at in halves: the whole left side, the whole right side, the bottom half, and the top half.

The Collective

The whole lower half (below the AC/DC line) is called the collective.

By spiritual age point, this bottom section covers the first forty-two years of life. These are the years people spend finding their place in the world. They do the things expected of them by their family, friends, neighbours, school, and (perhaps) religion, and they feel they are part of the collective identity in their community.

People with the majority of their planets in the collective are happy within their own environment, and they follow other people's expectations of them because they need the security of their family and friends around them. They will be happy to make a significant contribution to their community, anything from working or volunteering at schools to running a local club, driving people here and there, etc. They strive to maintain the continuity of the collective community by being an active member of it however they are able.

In this book, the collective refers to planets that are below the horizon line. People with planets here use them in the community, and their lifelong work is often unseen on the world's stage—they are not in the public eye.

Individual Thinking

The whole upper section (above the AC/DC line) is called the individual thinking area.

Those with a lot of planets up here think for themselves and do not necessarily believe what they are told—they prefer to find their own answers. They are not trapped by other people's expectations of them. People with planets in this sector don't want to get involved with the bottom of the chart; they perceive the collective community as noisy and busy and chaotic.

People with most of their planets at the top of the chart like being alone to think, learn, or write. A university professor is an ideal example of the individual thinking section of the chart: They spend most of their time alone in an office, writing an article for an elite magazine or editing specialised books. Occasionally, they dip into the collective community by teaching a few classes, but they always return to the peace of the individual thinking area.

For the purposes of this book, this is the area above the horizon line. It refers to those whose life path (via Saturn, the sun, and the nodes) is destined to be seen by the world.

The "Me" Side

The whole left side of the chart, from the IC to MC, is known as the Me area.

When a chart has most of the planets on the left, Me side, the individual will not need other people. They are happy alone and quite self-contained, maybe even reclusive or hermit-like. People with a scattering of planets all down the left side may choose workplaces that are away from the public eye, like a prison or hospital, or they might decide to enter religious or spiritual institutions. They may choose work that takes them away for long periods of time or prefer to work from home or in solo occupations. Alternatively, they might have ordinary jobs but ideally have an office to themselves. They will spend most of their free time on their own.

They might choose not to marry or have children. Certainly, if they do, it will not be easy for them to relate to their partner or children. Their partner may be responsible for a lot of the day-to-day care and running of the household. If every personal planet is on the Me side of the chart, this means the individual will have a problem relating to others. The moon here, especially, means emotional bonding with others will be difficult.

The "Others" Side

The entire right side of the chart, from the IC to MC, is known as the Others area.

Someone with most of their planets on the right-hand side desperately needs other people. What other people think, say, and expect from them will form the whole structure of their life.

Someone with all their planets here will be unable to function alone. They will marry or take partners early in life, and if a partner leaves, they may feel suicidal. Without other people, they are lost and have no inner resources.

Spiritual Age Point

Each house of a birth chart covers seven years of someone's life. Think of the astrological chart like a clock, with the line denoting the start of the ascendant/rising sign as the start of that clock, and work around the chart counterclockwise. Thus, the 1st house starts at birth and lasts until seven years old, the 2nd house covers seven to fourteen years old, the 3rd house covers fourteen to twenty-one years old, the 4th house covers twenty-one to twenty-eight years old, the 5th house covers twenty-eight to thirty-five years old, the 6th house covers thirty-five to forty-two years old, and so on. Until the age of forty-two, a person will be passing, by age point, through the bottom six houses of the chart. If we take into account the meaning of each house, it's easier to understand this idea.

It is not necessary to know your spiritual age point, but it is certainly helpful, especially at times of crisis in your life. If you feel stuck or unsure of what to do, or if you reach a point where a tough decision has to be made, it helps to understand the energies around you. The age point is often predictive too. For example, if you feel that life has ground to a halt and seems to be going nowhere, check your age point. For example, it could be that you are going through a house that has no planets in it. This is a message from the universe that this lull in your life is the time to take stock of your beliefs and restore your energy. In other words, use the slow period rather than fighting against it. Not every stage of life needs to be active and busy; we all need quiet times in which to take stock.

Let's look at the spiritual age point in more detail.

From Birth to Age Forty-Two

The moment we are born, our ascendant (AC) is set. So, that is where we start. For the first seven years of life we are passing, by age point, through the 1st house, so we express the qualities of the sign in the 1st house. We are children demanding our needs be met (reflected by the ruler of the

1st house being Aries). We go through the 2nd house at ages seven to fourteen, and it is during this time we seek nurturing and security (2nd/Taurus). From the ages of fourteen to twenty-one, we pursue education more fully and start to express ourselves as individuals (3rd/Gemini). From ages twenty-one to twenty-eight, it is common to want to set up our own home (4th/Cancer). From twenty-eight to thirty-five, we learn more fully how to express ourselves in our own way; we may have children too (5th/Leo). By the time we pass through the 6th house at ages thirty-five to forty-two, we are actively serving others (Virgo), usually because we have taken on responsibilities and have to buckle down and attend to them.

During all these years, we are also learning to become part of the community and finding out how to take our place in the world. This is because the bottom half of the chart is the collective area.

Ages 42–84

After the 6th house, continue to count every house as seven years. Now, we are moving towards the top of the chart. The 7th house (ages forty-two to forty-nine) concerns our chosen relationships and how we relate to others. Generally, by this stage, we are endeavouring to adjust our feelings and thoughts on how to handle our life partner so we can live harmoniously. If a partnership isn't working, this is when it becomes obvious, and perhaps another search is begun now that we know ourselves and better understand what we want in a partner. This time is also known as the midlife crisis point: We are moving from the collective, where we do what's expected of us, to the higher part of the chart, where we make decisions for ourselves.

As we pass through each house, we are drawn to think about those aspects of life. The astrological sign in that house will colour our thoughts and actions, and any planet we pass will be more fully activated. For example, let's say your 8th house is in Capricorn. You will be more focussed on wealth and status during those years, and you will certainly act in a more traditional manner. If you also have Mars in the 8th, its energy will be activated when you pass over it by age point, making you more proactive and driven.

The 8th house covers ages forty-nine to fifty-six, the 9th ages fifty-six to sixty-three, and we reach the MC (10th/Capricorn) at age sixty-three. By this stage, we often have attained the top of our career ladder or will soon. We continue through the 10th house until age seventy. We are then asked to join with others of like mind and ability in the 11th house (Aquarius, ages seventy to seventy-seven). After that, we start to consider our own mortality and the meaning of our entire life as we pass through the 12th house (ruled by Pisces, ages seventy-seven to eighty-four).

After age eighty-four, we come full circle and reach the AC again. By this point, it is likely we have retired from active life, and some of us will become dependent on others again—the second childhood, as it is called. We might soon need help with the basics of life. Certainly, as we age, we will need help from friends, family, and the community to see us through the physical restraints of old age, so we return to the bottom of the chart again.

To work out exactly where you are in your chart by age point, simply count from the start of the nearest house. For example, if you are twenty-nine, go to the start of the 5th house, which begins at age twenty-eight. Then, count the degrees between the 5th and 6th houses and divide that number by seven. If there are 28 degrees, dividing that number by seven would give you four. This means that you are progressing four degrees per year. So, you would count 4 degrees from the start of the 5th house, and that is exactly where you would be at twenty-nine. To see where you would be at thirty, you would count another 4 degrees, and so on.

The North Nodes

The north nodes show the area of life (the house) where we are meant to learn the most lessons in this lifetime. The astrological sign the north nodes are in provides more detailed information.

The North Nodes by House

Most astrologers believe that if we follow the path our north node indicates, we will find happiness and fulfilment. Although it certainly does indicate our cosmic life direction, in my experience, we are not particularly drawn to this house (area of life) unless we have other personal planets in the same house. However, by the end of our lives, most of us will have accepted certain aspects of the north node house, though it is rare for someone to accept it entirely. I believe this is because a house covers many aspects, and it's hard to know which we need to adopt. In any case, it's best to follow the path life leads us down, as we will always end up where we need to be.

The theory of the nodes is that we spent our previous lifetime in the opposite house, which is the south node area. There is no symbol on a chart to indicate the south node, but it's a point exactly opposite the north node. Sometimes it is drawn as a reversed north node symbol.

Because we have past experience in the south node area of life, we are comfortable and happy in our south node house. In this lifetime, though, we have to move to the opposite house if we can. It's likely we will always be more comfortable in our south node area, but life is about growth, and growth is often uncomfortable.

Here is a brief overview of what the node placements mean. There is a more detailed explanation in my book *Birth Chart Interpretation Plain & Simple*.

North Node in the 1st House
(South Node in the 7th House)

The 1st house and its opposite, the 7th, are all about relationships. In your past life, you formed a long-term relationship and developed the ability to compromise and share. In fact, you came to rely on your partner totally. Therefore, you come into this life with an easy ability to form lasting relationships. It's likely you feel lost without a partner, so you may choose unsuitable partners because you need to be with someone to feel whole.

In this life, your north node is in the 1st house, so you are being asked to begin to think of yourself and to become more independent of partners.

North Node in the 2nd House
(South Node in the 8th House)

You come from the 8th house. This means that in the last life, you relied on other people to provide for your needs; it's possible that you even accepted another person's values and gave up your own beliefs.

In this life, which is usually very successful in material terms, you are being called on to take responsibility for yourself and your actions so that you do not have to rely on anyone else.

North Node in the 3rd House
(South Node in the 9th House)

You come from the 9th house of wisdom and esoteric thought. In the last life, you would have spent many years alone in search of answers, which allowed you to form your personal view of the world and the purpose of life.

In this life, you're being asked to mix with everyone so that you can pass on the wisdom you learnt. You can do this in any way that feels right as long as it falls within the 3rd house: teaching, lecturing, writing, singing, preaching, etc.

North Node in the 4th House
(South Node in the 10th House)

With this node position, all the lessons in your last life were about the 10th house. You had a position of authority in your career, so now you feel comfortable being in control and managing others.

This time, though, you are being asked to go to the 4th house of home and family. This life is about looking after people, and you won't receive recognition from the outside world. Instead of controlling relationships, which you became used to, you are now being asked to have feeling/serving relationships.

North Node in the 5th House
(South Node in the 11th House)

This position of the north node means you come from the 11th house, which is where groups of intelligent people make decisions on behalf of others. In the previous life, you probably had a high-profile position and mixed with powerful people.

In this lifetime, you are being asked to mix with everyone, to learn to rub shoulders with all sorts of people down in the collective area. Basically, you need to bring your expertise right to the people who could benefit from it.

North Node in the 6th House
(South Node in the 12th House)

The 6th house is all about service to others, which involves hard work, literally rolling up your sleeves, and being of use. Very often, it is unsung work behind the scenes.

Moving towards the 6th house during this lifetime won't be easy because your comfort zone is the 12th house, a place of quiet retreat. However, the beliefs you formed during your previous contemplative lifetime now have to be put into practice in the 6th house through hard work.

North Node in the 7th House
(South Node in the 1st House)

Your last life dealt with the concerns of the 1st house, so you learnt how to be independent and an individual. You probably lived alone or were very detached from relationships that asked anything of you.

In this lifetime, you feel you don't need other people and can manage perfectly well as you are. But the 7th house is the place of long-term, one-on-one relationships and marriage. It is about compromise and balance and taking the needs of another into account. This is your challenge: learning how to relate to another and the compromises involved.

North Node in the 8th House
(South Node in the 2nd House)

You come into this life with a secure belief in your own values and abilities. In the last life, you stood on your own two feet and managed to create a safe, secure environment for yourself and your loved ones. It is likely you accumulated wealth and property too.

The north node in the 8th house means that in this life, you have to start learning how to rely on others. It won't be easy to hand over control to others, but you have to learn to take even though you've been used to giving.

North Node in the 9th House
(South Node in the 3rd House)

In the last life you believed, without question, what your teachers and other people in authority told you. You didn't explore the deeper meanings and issues because you assumed they were right.

With this north node position, you are being asked to move away from collective thinking and to search for your own answers, to learn how to make up your own mind and not necessarily believe what other people tell you. The 9th house is the house of philosophical thought and ideas.

North Node in the 10th House
(South Node in the 4th House)

In the previous life, you devoted your entire life to your family. What they believed defined your goals.

In this life, you have to set your own goals, which means standing up to your family and leaving the nest. It will be scary not having that emotional or financial support, but your task in this life is to pursue your own goals and find your unique path in life via your career.

North Node in the 11th House
(South Node in the 5th House)

You come from the 5th house, where you would have had a lot of close contact with people from all walks of life. This probably involved random love affairs and children by different partners. There is a reason for this: You were learning about human relationships and the close connections between people.

In this lifetime, you are being asked to go towards the 11th house, the place of humanitarian ideals and values. You will find yourself becoming more discriminating in your choice of friends as life progresses. Your task is to improve the lives of others through selective groups and associations, to use your previous experience and knowledge of the collective to enhance the lives of those less fortunate.

North Node in the 12th House
(South Node in the 6th House)

In your past life, you saw to the needs of others, willingly serving them. In this life, you'll still carry that desire to help people in practical ways, and you are not at all worried about having to undertake physical work. However, in this life you are meant to take a step back and to meditate in order to find your own spiritual meaning. This means doing less hands-on work and letting others take care of themselves, even though it comes so naturally to you.

The North Node by Astrological Sign

The astrological sign the north node occupies is also important. It shows how to go about adapting to the north node house.

North Node in Aries (South Node in Libra)

Coming from the sign of Libra, which deals with partnerships, means you easily see all sides of an issue, making it almost impossible for you to reach a decision. You think what other people want is what you want because keeping the peace and compromising is second nature to you. You try to please all people all of the time.

But in this lifetime, with your north node in Aries, you have to learn to put yourself first. Life circumstances will force you to assume a more independent role in this life in one way or another, which may mean not having relationships or not allowing them to become your primary motivation. In this life, you need space to develop who you are.

North Node in Taurus (South Node in Scorpio)

Scorpio is a deeply emotional, passionate, and suspicious sign, so it's likely you enjoy creating dramatic situations. You love drama, and when things get dull, you'll do things just to stir everyone up! Your actions may be based on jealousy, suspicion, or just plain boredom.

In this life, you will learn it's okay to just be, and that others are genuine and do not always have bad motives. You'll come to see the best in people rather than assume the worst, and you'll learn to stop rocking the boat just because you like life to be dramatic.

North Node in Gemini (South Node in Sagittarius)

You have a lot of wisdom from your last life, so now you find it hard to relate to people on an ordinary level. You probably feel out of step with society. But, despite feeling this way, verbalising and confessing these feelings is quite hard.

In this life, you'll learn how to relate to others and how to accept the traditions that are necessary when people live in a cohesive society. It's likely you lived alone in a past life, but now you have to live with others in the collective community so you can pass your wisdom on to others.

North Node in Cancer (South Node in Capricorn)

Your south node in Capricorn gives you knowledge and expertise of being in charge of others, of being out in the world forging a career that brings rewards and status. It's possible that in your last life, you ran your own business. Respect and recognition are important to you.

In this lifetime, you are being asked to look after your family, to let go of grand ambitions in life, to learn to be more humble, to let the world go by without actively taking part, and to concentrate on the needs of those closest to you; in effect, to be more Cancerian.

North Node in Leo (South Node in Aquarius)

Aquarius is the sign of many friendships, but close, personal relationships are challenging. Because this is your past life comfort zone, it's likely you are cool and detached in personal matters, unmaterialistic, and non-judgemental.

In this lifetime, though, you have to become more personal, as you are being asked to move towards the sign of Leo in the collective and mix with people from all walks of life. This also means having close relationships. Instead of holding yourself at a distance, you need to learn how to be part of the crowd, how to stand in the limelight, and how to be a spokesperson.

North Node in Virgo (South Node in Pisces)

You come from the sign of Pisces, which means you have great compassion and understanding. You generally forgive everyone for everything.

In this lifetime, you will learn to stop taking on the burdens of others. It is important to discern between those you can help and those who will drain you. You'll start thinking more like a Virgo as time goes on. Virgos still serve others, but they do so more practically. They attend to details, organise, and work hard. It is through physical work you will find your true self in this life.

North Node in Libra (South Node in Aries)

An Aries south node means that in the last life, you were a courageous, impulsive action-taker.

Now, though, you are being asked to follow the opposite path. This lifetime it is all about learning to compromise, to share, and to focus on the needs of others— to move from Aries qualities to Libra qualities. Lessons will be found in all sorts of partnerships: business partnerships, romantic relationships, family dynamics, etc.

North Node in Scorpio (South Node in Taurus)

You came into this life with strength, determination, and absolutely fixed ideas. You have the ability to work hard and accumulate wealth through your own efforts.

Possessions bring you a sense of security. This is your Taurus south node in action.

In this lifetime, you are being asked to experience life through the sign of Scorpio. Scorpio opens the door to new emotions and feelings, to passions that are not always physical. The security you so desire may be taken away, and instead of providing for others, you may find that you have to rely on others.

North Node in Sagittarius (South Node in Gemini)

Gemini is your south node, which means you are friendly, chatty, and dislike too much detail. It's likely you avoid commitment or being tied down to a time, place, or person.

In this lifetime, you have to move to a higher level because the sign of Sagittarius is the sign of esoteric thought. You will be required to deeply look into subjects, especially the meaning of existence. At some stages, you might be more isolated from others than you would like, but this gives you the time and space to form new ideas.

North Node in Capricorn (South Node in Cancer)

A Cancer south node means that in the last life, you looked after people, most likely your own family. You are nurturing and caring and always willing to do things for other people.

However, in this lifetime you are being asked to find a career. This won't be easy at first, because you won't feel ambitious or even interested in the outside world—your family is everything to you. Gradually, though, you'll realise your family doesn't need you quite as much. There will be a sense of freedom in not having to be all things to all people, leaving you time to express your own identity through a career. Because your north node is in the sign of Capricorn, whose ruler is Saturn, this career often comes later in life after many setbacks.

North Node in Aquarius (South Node in Leo)

Leo is the sign of royalty, so you come into this life with the feeling that you are special. It will be hard to throw off this attitude. In the last life, you were definitely in a leadership role that called for admiration and praise from others.

So, in this lifetime, you probably have an innate feeling that you are better than everyone else, and you prefer to mix with people you perceive to be your social equals. However, over time, you'll start seeing the world as full of equals, and you will learn to be more Aquarian. You will be able to put friendship before love and will be less ego-driven.

North Node in Pisces (South Node in Virgo)

Your past life in Virgo endowed you with a need for structure, rules, and regulations, but the world is a disorganised place. Trying to tidy everything, organise people, and bring structure where there is none will exhaust you, perhaps even make you ill.

In this lifetime, you'll learn how to go with the flow. You will realise it is not your responsibility to keep picking up the pieces. Your north node sign of Pisces has nothing to do with logic or reason and everything to do with instinct and intuition. You will learn to stand back and let life go on.

To Write to the Author

If you wish to contact the author or would like more information about this book, please write to the author in care of Llewellyn Worldwide Ltd. and we will forward your request. Both the author and publisher appreciate hearing from you and learning of your enjoyment of this book and how it has helped you. Llewellyn Worldwide Ltd. cannot guarantee that every letter written to the author can be answered, but all will be forwarded. Please write to:

Andrea Taylor
℅ Llewellyn Worldwide
2143 Wooddale Drive
Woodbury, MN 55125-2989

Please enclose a self-addressed stamped envelope for reply, or $1.00 to cover costs. If outside the U.S.A., enclose an international postal reply coupon.

Many of Llewellyn's authors have websites with additional information and resources. For more information, please visit our website at http://www.llewellyn.com.